MW01520091

The Project Management Imperative

The Project Management Imperative

Mastering the Key Survival Skill for the Twenty-first Century Organization

David Wirick, PMP, CMA
with Gretchen Bond, PMP
Foreword by David J. Hansen, PhD, PMP

iUniverse, Inc.
New York Lincoln Shanghai

The Project Management Imperative
Mastering the Key Survival Skill for the Twenty-first Century Organization

Copyright © 2005 by Babbage-Simmel & Associates, Inc.

All rights reserved. No part of this book may be used or reproduced by any means, graphic, electronic, or mechanical, including photocopying, recording, taping or by any information storage retrieval system without the written permission of the publisher except in the case of brief quotations embodied in critical articles and reviews.

iUniverse books may be ordered through booksellers or by contacting:

iUniverse
2021 Pine Lake Road, Suite 100
Lincoln, NE 68512
www.iuniverse.com
1-800-Authors (1-800-288-4677)

"PMI," "PMBOK," and "PMP" are registered trademarks of the Project Management Institute, Inc.

ISBN-13: 978-0-595-37226-3 (pbk)
ISBN-13: 978-0-595-81624-8 (ebk)
ISBN-10: 0-595-37226-0 (pbk)
ISBN-10: 0-595-81624-X (ebk)

Printed in the United States of America

To our clients,
who graciously give us both their trust
and the chance to learn with them.

ACKNOWLEDGMENTS

We are grateful to our colleagues at Babbage Simmel for their support and encouragement. We are particularly appreciative of the editing and comments provided by David Hansen and Andrew Lavinsky. We are also especially grateful to Louis Maani, who believed in us and in this book, and who believes in serving clients and humanity.

CONTENTS

FOREWORD

Today's project managers have the opportunity to choose from a growing body of project management literature. What makes this book different? While most project management books address the project manager's needs, this book is focused on the needs of the organization. On these pages, the organization is the client, the customer, and the patient. *The Project Management Imperative* is about how to build a healthy and productive organization that can make effective use of project management.

Many authors have attempted to show how to manage a project in an organization. Wirick and Bond present a model of how to manage an organization that embraces projects.

They provide a comprehensive model for applying project management knowledge and processes to organizations and also supply a guide to the organizational change of the enterprise as a whole.

This book addresses four critical areas of concern. First, this book addresses how to identify and deal with elements of change, including barriers to change in managing projects effectively. The issues of silos and turf lines that keep functional organizations from becoming nimble organizations that are able to assemble and reassemble project teams and accumulate lessons learned are presented here. Strategic elements needed to resolve these issues are also presented.

Second, this book asks what professional skills we need to build within our organizations, how we do that, and what we can expect from training programs. Training is not hard to find. Training that makes a difference is.

The third question addressed by the book is what software and enterprise solutions are available to the organization that embraces a project culture, and how you choose these solutions.

Finally, this book answers a fourth important question: what types of organizational structures do we need to have in place in order to capture, utilize, and cultivate a "project culture?" Anyone who has ever tried to change an organization has faced resistance. This book presents three key organizational structures that are critical to the process and permanence of a project management improvement initiative.

Wirick and Bond bring years of experience in project management, organizational change, and training to this book, and they present realistic scenarios.

The language is down-to-earth. They show us that a project culture is something we can build, and they show us how we can accomplish it.

This book shows how to introduce project management into an organization and to affect the organization's capacity. It will become a reference book for project managers, organizations, and authors for years to come.

David J. Hansen, PhD, PMP
Executive Director, Organizational Innovation and Learning
Babbage Simmel
Columbus, Ohio
October 2005

CHAPTER 1

Project Management and the Twenty-first Century Organization

In an environment that requires flexibility, responsiveness, and intense competition for resources, the traditional, hierarchical, and internally focused organization no longer fits. It's too slow and too rigid, and it's rapidly becoming extinct in the "take no prisoners" markets of the twenty-first century.

In response to the needs of the times, a new, faster-moving organizational model is emerging among organizations that are positioning themselves for success. This new model is sometimes called the virtual organization or the network organization. Though some organizations are better suited to the new model than others, nearly every organization can employ at least some of the principles of the new model to become more competitive and effective.

This book examines a fundamental building block for organizations operating in these challenging times—project management. This proven tool provides a solid base for those organizations attempting to meet the challenges and apply the new organizational models required. Successful project management can serve as the engine for mandatory and constant innovation.

Project management will be central to the success of modern organizations for the following reasons:

- The need for more flexible, accountable, and less-hierarchical organizational models
- The need to create a better balance between process improvement and project management
- The failure of traditional project management

Each of these requirements for effective project management will be discussed in this chapter.

The New, Mandatory Organizational Structure

For decades, the principal functions of managers were to effectively plan and control the resources at their disposal. They were rewarded for plotting a path for their organizations and for deploying resources to accomplish results. To make things happen in traditional environments, control was centralized and subordinates were constrained. Even the term *subordinate* connoted a management style that relied on "subordinating" the wisdom of others to the will of the manager, who was regarded as wiser than those within his or her span of control.

With the objective of producing desirable products at the least possible cost, managers attempted to make constant, incremental improvements in processes, reduce the probability of mistakes, and build policies and procedures that could effectively govern the organization. Decision making was consolidated to standardize processes and lower the total cost of production.

> Every organization is involved in a process of wrenching change. Those that can master that change will survive. Those that can't master it, won't.

In those traditional, hierarchical organizations, the majority of human resources were characterized as employees, the organization utilized its own resources to meet customer demands, and resources were seen as interchangeable or replaceable. There were strong incentives to build permanent structures and capacity and to create management empires by increasing a manager's span of control. For employees, lifetime employment was expected.

Teams were formed from the organization's own internal resources. Innovation, though desired in theory, was rarely rewarded and tightly controlled. Speed, flexibility, and competitiveness were sacrificed for predictability, safety, and a semblance of control. In an economy dominated by manufacturing and other repeatable-process industries, the traditional organizational structure was stable and positioned for long-term, steady growth.

In the twenty-first century, the old economy, the old stability, and the old sense of security are gone. Market competition has become global as opposed to local, regional, or national, and even the stability of government programs and employment is being eroded by the competition for scarce public resources.

To meet the requirements of the new age, a new organizational form is emerging.[1] It is an organizational model forged by the heat of competition, the scarcity of resources, and the motivational needs of the knowledge workers whose talents drive the new economy. Organizations that have embraced this new model have the following characteristics:

- They are built to support the client-facing elements of the organization (e.g., sales and delivery) rather than to sustain the organizational hierarchy.
- They eliminate layers of management.
- They rely more on personal accountability, employee initiative, and an entrepreneurial ethic.
- They are designed to increase intra-organizational and inter-organizational interactivity.
- Their management realizes that knowledge is the most important asset of the organization.
- They are built on flexible, loose organizational platforms with constantly evolving partnerships and alliances.
- Their management attempts to force patterns of mature behavior.
- They increase the ability of the organization to innovate and get things done.
- They create internal markets for valued resources.

The new model is not restricted to high-tech organizations or service firms; nearly every organization, business or government, is now being pressured to consider its adoption. There may be organizations that wholly adopt it to the exclusion of any other organizational models, while others will take elements of the model and blend it with other, more traditional organizational arrangements. It will, however, ultimately affect every manager and every organization to some degree.

> Because project management requires the creation of project teams that can accomplish things within a short time, it provides a tool for increasing organizational flexibility and responsiveness.

---

[1] There are many sources describing the new economy and its requirements for organizations. A good one is Don Tapscott, *The Digital Economy*. New York: McGraw-Hill, 1996.

The principles of project management align very closely with the needs of the new organization in a number of ways. First, projects are performed by temporary teams that may bring together heterogeneous groups of professionals across great distances. Similarly, the new organizational model requires that organizations create and disband alliances to fit the shifting needs of the organization. Project management is built around temporary, flexible linkages.

Projects are necessary for the creation of change, which is a constant requirement for successful organizations in these tumultuous times. Project management is also ideal for stakeholder integration, an increasing challenge in complex environments and markets.

Today, organizations tend to be more geographically dispersed than in the past. Project management is outcome oriented and ideal for the management of geographically remote staff. In addition, projects often extend outside the boundaries of the performing organization and are sometimes undertaken because the performing organization is incapable of creating the necessary results. The new organizational model often extends beyond the traditional boundaries of the organization.

Well-managed projects established clear outcomes and accountability, two characteristics that are sometimes lacking in traditional organizations. The new organizations need to employ technology to create rapid, sometimes temporary, communications systems. Projects establish temporary communication networks with a wide array of stakeholders and employ a variety of communications tools.

Some of the best, new organizations can even be described as "projectized." That is, they use projects not only as a means to accomplish results but also build their structure around those projects. In those organizations, project managers (though often called by other titles) are among the most highly rewarded and relied-upon professional staff.

The Balance between Processes and Projects

The new organization also requires different management strategies. Whereas traditional organizations employed process control and process engineering to build cost advantages, the new organization requires a greater emphasis on project management to assure the effectiveness of short-term initiatives and the rapidly changing alliances that characterize them.

It can be argued that traditional organizations were too "process-centric." That is, organizations staked out a line of business and a market or, in the case of government organizations, a mission and a set of programs. Success was measured by the ability to create processes that could deliver predictable products and outcomes efficiently. Management tools were established and applied to continuously improve those processes. They included TQM, CQI, reengineering, Six Sigma, and other versions of process control.

> No organization should focus on projects or processes to the exclusion of the other. There has to be an effective balance between the two, but, in these demanding and fast-paced times, we need to shift our emphasis toward project management.

Incremental change in processes was the norm, and changes in mission, customers, or lines of business were fairly rare. Managers attempted to predict change and control it.

Today, change is a constant, gut-wrenching fact of organizational existence. Managers today need tools that can embrace change and provide some measure of order amid the chaos. Fortunately, project management has matured to the point that effective application is within the grasp of every organization, no matter what its size.

As will be discussed at length later in this book, there is a clear, synergistic link between projects and processes, and no organization can survive without a commitment to improving both. In an era of constant change, project management may require a greater emphasis, given its role in enabling change.

The Failure of Traditional Project Management

Even though project management has clear, positive benefits for organizations, it has not reached its current prominence because of its close fit to the needs of modern organizations. Project management has received the attention it deserves in recent years because most organizations are recognizing that they are not very good at managing team-based, temporary work (projects). A host of statistics demonstrate that money is wasted on projects, that they are often late, and that the outcomes that they were designed to achieve are often not delivered.[2]

> In today's competitive marketplace, no organization can continue to deliver poor project results without putting its survival at risk.

---

[2] See among others The Standish Group at www.standishgroup.com.

Worse, nearly every organization can identify its failed projects, which have resulted in poor morale, disappointed customers, lost revenue, missed opportunities, ineffective processes, and a whole host of other problems. With enough failed projects, organizations can quickly lose market relevance. In addition, most organizations operate at such low levels of project management maturity that their project management methods and tools are ad hoc and invented on the fly. Their project management maturity is at the lowest level on most maturity assessments, and they struggle to identify projects, have little or no criteria for judging success or failure, wear out their staff with an endless stream of project crises, and follow each project with an attempt to assign blame.

We simply have to do better. Those organizations that continue to manage projects poorly will be challenged in the new environment. Those that improve their ability to manage projects will achieve a competitive advantage over those that don't.

The Case for Project Management

Project management is both a method for accomplishing results within fixed time and budget limits and a strategic tool for organizational advancement. Today, much of the important work of organizations is accomplished within projects. Those projects include new product development, customized client service, organizational change initiatives, process improvement, and a host of other initiatives in engineering, research, marketing, corporate governance, finance, human resources, manufacturing, and other disciplines.

Project management is based on solid management principles that can be of value to any organization. Those principles include the following:

- A focus on measurable results delivered within the budget assigned and the time required
- Clear responsibility for outcomes and extensive involvement of project team members in project planning
- A scope of work that is clearly defined and agreed upon
- Careful risk management
- Clear identification of stakeholders, including customers
- The creation of effective, temporary project teams
- A bias toward action
- The ability to transcend organizational boundaries
- Proactive communications with internal and external stakeholders.

Creating a solid project management capacity in any organization is a challenge, but it is a challenge that has been met by many organizations and can be met by almost any who apply a comprehensive approach to change.

Organizations like the Project Management Institute (PMI®) have created and documented standards for project management that can be applied by nearly any organization and have already provided demonstrable results. Standards may be scaled to any size organization or size project. They demonstrate that project management is both a method for accomplishing results within fixed time and budget limits and a strategic tool for organizational advancement. It is both effective and achievable.

The Focus of This Book

There are many books that help individual managers get better at the application of project management tools and techniques. There are also books that examine the role of the PMO, a common but sometimes ill-considered approach to making project management work for the organization.

This book is different. It is designed to provide a comprehensive set of solutions to help organizations increase their capacity to manage projects effectively. It is focused on the needs of senior managers, human resource managers, those who manage project management offices, and those project managers who understand that the entire organization must be empowered and aligned if project management is to realize its full potential. Though improving the skills of individual project managers is one step in organizational transformation and will be described here, it is just one step of many that are required if the organization is to embrace project management and become as nimble and effective as the times require.

Though the processes and skills of professional project management can have an impact on individual projects and individual project managers, project management can only reach its full potential if it is adopted by the organization as a whole and integrated fully into the operations of the organization. In this manner, the organization can develop comprehensive project management capacity and enhance organizational learning.

The organizational building blocks of successful project management initiatives described in this book are as follows:

- The decision to invest in project management
- Creating learning programs that are cost-effective and targeted
- Development of project management skills and those skills that complement project management

- Adoption of a project management methodology
- Choice of a project management tool
- Alignment of the organizational structure to the goals of project management
- Creation of a project management community of practice and culture of project management
- Measuring the progress of the organization in improving its project management maturity

In Chapter 2, we'll describe the organizational impediments to getting project management right and detail a comprehensive approach for improving project management capacity. In Chapter 3, we'll create the elements of a comprehensive change strategy, including the development of the business case for the project management initiative and strategies for getting the organization committed to a project management initiative.

We'll then address the challenges of developing the necessary project management skill sets. Chapter 4 will describe the changing expectations for training programs and describe effective methods for skill development. In Chapter 5, we'll examine the skill domains for effective project management, the necessary skill sets, and the special need for "soft" skills and ancillary skills.

Having examined the "people" side of project management capacity, in Chapter 6 we'll look at the need for a customized project management methodology for the organization, the necessary components of one, and the special need for project selection and prioritization processes. Chapter 7 is dedicated to the role and choice of project management software with a special focus on the plusses and minuses of enterprise project management solutions.

In Chapter 8, we'll look at the organizational structures necessary for project management success and examine the role of project management offices and the challenges to their success. Chapter 9 describes the importance of knowledge management and continuity management in sustaining the project management capacity of the organization, elements of capacity development that are often overlooked. We'll take an especially close look at communities of practice, a vital tool for dissemination of project management knowledge and the development of the capacity of the organization to continue to learn when the formal training is done.

In Chapter 10, we will conclude by examining the barriers to change related to the project management initiative and present several effective change management tools. We'll focus on moving people beyond their comfort zones and limiting adversity and unintended sabotage of the initiative. While this book is designed to address the need to integrate project management into the culture and operations of the organization, much of what we say here can be applied to the introduction of any significant change.

Appendix 1 presents a short-form tool for assessing your organization's project management maturity. There are more comprehensive tools available for conducting that assessment, but this method is fast and provides useful data and an introduction to the components required for increased maturity.

Appendix 2 explores and explains the major mathematical tools available for evaluating projects and prioritizing projects.

In addition, there a several case studies spread throughout the book to provide real-world application of the concepts presented.

Figure 1.1 describes the major deliverables of the comprehensive approach and the chapters in which those deliverables are described. As these deliverables are produced within the initiative to improve the organization's project management capacity, the project management maturity of the organization will increase.

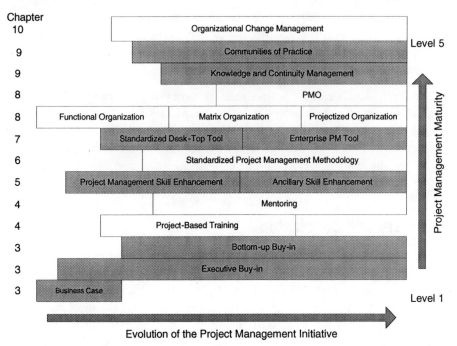

Figure 1.1
Major Deliverables of the Project Management Improvement Initiative

The framework presented here conforms to *A Guide to the Project Management Body of Knowledge (PMBOK® Guide)—Third Edition*, but it also introduces tools and concepts that extend beyond that important source of project management standards. The *PMBOK® Guide* addresses organizational issues in only a few pages. This book extends the information presented there with more detailed information about the organizational application of project management.

A one-size-fits-all approach to project management capacity development is not effective. Each organization needs to craft an approach to project management that meets its needs and is built around its internal operations and external environment. Not all organizations should aspire to reach Level 5 on project management maturity models, which are described later. Achieving that level is expensive and time-consuming, but nearly all organizations can improve the way they apply project management tools and techniques and seek better project outcomes.

> The first step in increasing the project management capability of your organization is not buying software or providing "one-time" training to managers. It's building a comprehensive project plan for the effort.

We also realize that most project management initiatives operate "under the gun" of senior managers who need to see rapid results. Though they might realize that it may take time to fully capture the benefits of effective project management, they need project performance on key projects now. For that reason, at the end of every relevant chapter we have also identified tips for "jump starting" your project management initiatives.

Summary and Conclusions

No organization operates in an ideal state. Instead, most exist in a state of uncertainty, confusion, fluidity, and stress. The people who work in them are not automatons or perfect employees. Organizations and people struggle and create conflict. They get stressed and burned out. They are skeptical and resistant to change. They don't listen to one another or adhere to policies and procedures in the way we expect them to. That is why each organization needs to develop a comprehensive, robust approach to project management that provides incentives and builds effective project management into the core and culture of the organization. That is what this book is designed to do.

Managers and organizations that have embarked on the journey to change the way they manage projects have, to some extent, begun the hero's quest. Like King Arthur, Perceval, and others who sought the Holy Grail, those managers will be challenged and sometimes frustrated. They will sometimes lose their way. They will at times question the meaning and relevance of their quest. But when they are done, they will have created fundamental change and positioned their organizations for long-term success in the fast-paced economy of the future.

CHAPTER 2

The Organizational Challenges to Effective Project Management

If project management is required for the modern, network organization and if there are books on managing projects, why can't we just buy a couple of project management books and start getting things done?

Obviously, it's not that easy. In the last chapter, we discussed the fact that no organization is ideal. Each is full of people with their own agendas, processes that are cumbersome, and communications channels that seem to be designed to frustrate people rather than inform them. Looking at organizations reminds us of the phenomenon of the dancing elephant, where the wonder is not that it dances so poorly, but that it dances at all.

In this chapter, we'll begin to look at how attempts to manage projects often bump into the real world of organizations. Before we identify strategies for making project management work, we'll take a quick look at why it usually doesn't.

What is a Project and How Are We Doing at Delivering Results?

Projects are temporary and designed to produce something unique. They should have a beginning and an end, though projects that seem to flow unimpeded and uncontrolled forever are common. They also produce unique results, which distinguishes them from operations or repeatable processes.

Projects are creative and drive change. If change is a constant and a requirement for survival, managing projects successfully is mandatory in order to cope with that change. Projects can be large or small; they can be accomplished by a single person or a 1000-person project team; they can last a week or for years.

> The survival of most organizations is dependent on projects. Unfortunately, most organizations are ill-prepared to succeed on these critical projects.

Traditionally, when we thought about projects, we thought about tangible activities like construction and research. Indeed, these are indeed projects, but today in a business environment projects can include such activities as the following:

- Introducing new products
- Flattening the organization
- Conducting consumer research
- Spinning off operations or merging with another organization
- Changing salary structures
- Creating a strategic plan
- Delivering specialized, customer-specific services
- Creating and implementing a plan to reduce costs or downsizing
- Acquiring financing
- Going public
- Improving processes
- Creating and implementing a program for improving morale and employee incentives
- Automating operations or upgrading systems
- Preparing the annual report
- Achieving regulatory compliance (e.g., Sarbanes-Oxley or HIPAA)
- Creating plans for responding to competitive pressures
- Conducting a public relations campaign
- Outsourcing or moving operations

In most organizations, there are more projects underway at any time than can be accounted for, managed, or even identified. They get started without having clearly delineated goals and without a clear scope or charter. Often projects expand or meander as additional deliverables get tacked on and the end date is pushed farther and farther away. Some projects don't matter much, but some of them do matter a lot.

> Most organizations have so many projects underway at any time that it's hard to identify them, much less prioritize them or assign managers to them.

Today, many organizations are often faced with "bet the company" projects—those that are driven by business imperatives.

Unfortunately, we generally have a poor record of delivering projects such as these successfully. Even though projects represent a substantial slice of the worldwide economy, statistics and experience confirm our relative incompetence at producing project results on time, on budget, and with the functionality and results the project was designed to produce.

There was a time when the statistics of project failure could be viewed without alarm. When resources were plentiful and organizations were growing, project inefficiencies were an accepted fact of organizational life. When the business environment moved more slowly, projects were of less strategic importance and carried less risk than they do now. The evidence now suggests that projects are becoming more complex, bigger, and more critical to organizational survival.

In a business environment that demands rapid change and an assured return on organizational investments, effective management of all sorts of projects including IT, construction, research, organizational change, product development, and product introduction is imperative. Organizations simply cannot continue to waste money on failed projects and cannot continue to deliver less than internal and external customers demand. For each organization, at every level, and for the health of the economy as a whole, we have to do better. We have to build organizational competence in project management and get our projects right.

> There are personal consequences, too, for project failures. Managers who can deliver project results will succeed, and those who can't, won't.

Fortunately, the evidence has shown that effective project management has the ability to reduce project costs and risks and improve project outcomes. Project management education is a growth industry as more and more organizations attempt to increase their project management capability and maturity.

The Problem with Organizations

Project management, though it can be employed to send a mission to the moon, is not rocket science. It shouldn't be that difficult for organizations to make it work.

The problem for most organizations isn't mastering the discipline of project management. *The problem is employing project management methods and tools in the real-life, hectic, day-to-day operations of organizations.* Employing effective project management capacity requires pervasive changes in organizations. As many managers can attest, introducing any new discipline into an organization, including project management, is not a simple endeavor.

Effective project management cannot be integrated into organizational operations with a one-shot expenditure. While training is important, an organization cannot create effective project management simply by buying a few training courses. Although it is useful, project management software doesn't perform miracles. It can't convert poor managers or poor project management processes into effective ones; nor can organizational project management competency be created overnight. Any organization making a serious commitment to better project management must expect to invest time and resources. Fortunately, as many organizations can attest, the investment can be worth the effort.

The challenges facing an organization attempting to make better use of project management are enormous. The attempt to improve project management may be frustrated because of these issues:

- Senior managers fail to understand the strategic importance of effective project management and fail to champion it in the organization.

- Organizational boundaries inhibit the ability of project managers to acquire the necessary resources and manage their teams effectively. (As budgets get tighter and workloads go up, managing resources is becoming a more visible organizational pain point and rationale for the application of better project management.)

- Employee turnover saps the project management skills of the organization and destroys organizational memory.

- The organization does not commit the necessary resources to the project management initiative.

- Organizations fail to adequately involve the users of the product of the project in project planning and design and deliver products that don't meet the needs of key stakeholders.

- Staff regards the project management initiative as just another management fad that will pass away in time.

- A lack of understanding of project management by senior managers prevents project managers from undertaking adequate project planning (i.e., they may demand immediate results from a project rather than allow for careful planning, which almost always pays off).

- Project accountability is not clearly assigned. (We'll talk later about the resistance of functional managers to assignment of responsibility to project managers.)

- Functional managers don't provide adequate numbers of staff to project managers, don't assign staff with the right capabilities, don't support those staff persons in their project work, and make demands on their time that prohibit project work. (One of the biggest threats to project team member effectiveness is the demand of their "real" job.)

- Employees acquire the technical skills of project management but don't acquire the more essential soft skills that make the difference between adequate and great project management.

- The lack of good project cost data and project accounting systems limits decision making.

- Project management training is a one-shot initiative that fails to create sustainable organizational learning.

- The wrong people are trained on the wrong skills for the needs of the organization.

- Project management is regarded as the exclusive province of a few managers, instead of a set of tools used by all managers and staff.

- Project requirements are assumed rather than clearly articulated. (There is no more dangerous statement than "we all just know what the scope of the project is." If the scope isn't written down, it's subject to multiple interpretations, and inevitably the project will fail to meet those multiple expectations.)

- There isn't a system in place to assure consistent project closure and the transmission of lessons learned in a usable format.

- A project management office, if established, fails to deliver the intended results because of a lack of authority or confusion about its role.

- Project managers aren't organizationally savvy and don't recognize organizational constraints and solutions.

- Project managers are assigned without experience in the appropriate knowledge domains of project management (i.e., understanding of the problem, expertise in the solution, ability to apply appropriate processes, and ability to manage the environment or context of the project).
- The organization doesn't employ consistent project management processes.
- A culture of project failure has been created by prior projects.
- Projects are not prioritized or too many projects are underway at one time.
- The organization doesn't utilize valid project selection methods.
- The ability to initiate a project is distributed to too many people in the organization.
- The organization places too much emphasis on project management tools or fails to utilize tools where appropriate. (Many organizations start their initiative to improve projects by purchasing software. If the organizational issues of project management aren't addressed, the software may convert to "shelfware.")
- The organization ignores troubled projects and doesn't have an early warning system for identifying at-risk projects.
- The organization hasn't developed methods for allowing mentoring of junior project managers by more experienced ones.

> Organizations seem to do all they can to avoid making the changes that are necessary for effective project management. They unwittingly create formidable obstacles to any attempt to improve project management.

Though these challenges are common, any one of them can handicap the ability of an organization to build a culture and track record of project success. With all of these challenges, it is a wonder that organizations have made as much headway as they have, and it is clear that most could do better if these challenges could be addressed.

In stable business and government environments that characterized the world economy in the aftermath of World War II, introducing project management capabilities into an organization would have been complicated enough. Now, the introduction of project management into an organization will need to occur at a wrenching time in the history of most organizations.

Today, a confluence of forces is combining to change nearly everything we know about how organizations are supposed to function. These forces are impacting organizations in many ways. They are impacting people, processes, and technology, and have created the "perfect storm" of organizational change. Any attempt to create effective change, including changing the way the organization manages projects, has to be as comprehensive and pervasive as the other forces that organizations are trying to cope with.

The Path to Success

The challenges we've just described can be enormous. Whether the organization is just getting its start in project management or is seeking to improve its project management maturity, a comprehensive plan for improving the project management capacity of the organization is required. At a minimum, that plan for the organization must include the following:

- Building the business case for project management
- Creating an organizational commitment to improve project management capability
- Implementing a strategy of simultaneous top-down and bottom-up project management integration
- Developing individual competencies in the four knowledge domains essential for project managers
- Adopting an organizational process and tools that ensure effective project management, including standardized project selection and prioritization methods
- Creating organizational structures that enhance project management, including the project management office
- Establishing and nurturing project management communities of practice and other structures that allow for ongoing organizational learning and knowledge management
- Driving organizational change

The elements of this comprehensive strategy are detailed in the next chapter and in the remainder of this book.

Though the processes and skills of professional project management can have an impact on individual projects and individual project managers, project management can only reach its full potential if it is adopted by the organization as a whole and integrated fully into the operations of the organization.

Only in this manner, the organization can develop comprehensive project management capacity and enhance organizational learning—two essential keys to the success of the modern, network organization.

Summary and Conclusions

Projects have moved front and center in the struggle for organizational survival and success. Organizations that get projects right have a greater chance of coping with rapid change and thriving in the new economy. Unfortunately, most organizations don't have strong records of project success.

The problem isn't that project management is too complicated or that its methods are too difficult to master. The problem is that project management often collides with the messy circumstances of most organizations, including the people who work there. Indeed, the organizational forces arrayed against the application of project management may not be surmountable without a comprehensive and aggressive plan. Introducing effective project management into an organization requires deep and lasting change. That change will be uncomfortable for most, and the initiaitve to improve project management, sensible as it may seem, is certain to confront adversity.

In the remainder of this book, we will build a plan for helping your organization achieve better project results. It will require some choices, processes, tools, and organizational changes, but it can be fun, and it will bring almost immediate value to your organization.

CHAPTER 3

A Comprehensive Approach to Building the Project Management Initiative

As we noted in the last chapter, improving organizational capacity to deliver successful projects requires a comprehensive program that attacks that challenge from a variety of vantage points and with a variety of tools. Unfortunately, many organizations have suffered from the results of a one-dimensional approach, of which there are several unsuccessful variations.

Sometimes an organization faced with complex, high risk projects and a poor track record of delivering results will attempt to improve its project management capability by purchasing project management software. It looks deceptively simple; the software is, after all, referred to as "project management" software. In truth, there is no such thing as project management software, but only software that will assist project managers. Having evaluated the promises made by various software tools and having made an investment in the software, its installation, and training on its use, those organizations stand back and watch in dismay as projects are managed in the same ineffective manner as before. Too often, the software converts to "shelfware" and sits unused.

At times, organizations assume that providing one-time training to a few managers will do the trick. That seems simple as well. All it requires is the identification of a few key managers to send out for training. Training programs are readily available and promise dramatic improvements. With this single strategy, short-term improvements might result, but without adequate organizational support and ongoing skill development, the trained managers will likely give up and return to management patterns that they are more familiar with. These managers may feel cheated and misled, and the project management initiative is filed away as just one more management fad that was supposed to change the organization.

> An initiative to improve project management requires a comprehensive project plan and a multi-dimensional approach.

As we will see later, software tools and staff training are useful and should not be ignored. But a more comprehensive approach is necessary if the investment in project management capacity development is to bear its full fruits. At a minimum, effective project management initiatives require the following:

- Building the business case for a project management improvement initiative
- The creation of an organization-wide commitment to improve project management capability
- A strategy of simultaneous top-down and bottom-up implementation
- The development of individual competencies in four knowledge domains essential for project managers
- The adoption of project management processes and procedures that ensure effective project management, including project selection and prioritization methods and a standard project lifecycle for similar projects
- The creation of organizational structures that enhance project management, including the project management office
- The establishment and nurturing of project management communities of practice and other structures that allow for ongoing organizational learning and knowledge management
- The facilitation of organizational change

Each of the elements of that comprehensive approach to project management capacity development is described in the remainder of this chapter. Table 3.1 at the close of this chapter illustrates the application of the model and identifies some of the steps that might be considered in its application.

Building the Business Case for Project Management Improvement

To some, the wisdom of an investment in project management may seem obvious. Most organizations are well aware of their project deficiencies and the pains that poor project management cause. But we should be able to justify and quantify the value of a project management improvement initiative, just like we are required to justify any other organizational initiatives/projects.

As we discussed in the previous section, effective application of project management tools and processes requires an organizational commitment to project management. That commitment must be organizational and financial and must extend from the top of the organization to the bottom.

> Though a project management initiative might sound like a good idea to us, we'll have to generate the numbers to justify the use of the organization's scarce resources.

In order to create a successful project management initiative, we need to address the following:

- We must present arguments that speak to the needs of those who will sponsor the initiative. We'll have to spend time determining what those needs are and reduce the number of assumptions we make about them.

- We must ensure that our message is not lost among the clutter of organizational communications. Our message must be compelling enough that it stands out.

- We need to present a message that will build excitement so that it can be sustained among the other competing needs and initiatives of the organization.

- We should build a good business case. If the initiative can't be shown to impact the bottom line, it won't (and shouldn't) get the support it needs.

In many organizations, the decision to invest in project management will require a detailed justification, and that proposed initiative will need to be compared to other potential initiatives. It will have to make sense on a business level, which may require the calculation of a return on investment (ROI) for the initiative, and it will have to demonstrate a better value than other initiatives in which the organization has the potential to invest.

To assist you to build that commercial case for project management, we will address the following:

- Identify the value of improving the project management capacity of the organization.

- Examine the challenges inherent in demonstrating the costs and benefits of improving project management.

- Build a "business case" for project management that includes both quantitative and qualitative indicators of value.

No project justification is perfect. The business case for project management, like any other organizational change initiative, will in part be driven by hard data that will appeal to the intellect of senior managers. A few senior managers will have been so traumatized and angered by project failures that they will take on a project management improvement initiative on faith, feeling at an emotional level that anything is better than the current state. Others will respond better to data. As a result, the best justifications for an initiative to improve the way the organization manages projects will include both quantitative and qualitative value projections.

Identifying the Potential Value of a Project Management Initiative

What kinds of benefits might an organization expect from improving the way it manages projects? Some benefits might be obvious, like fewer project failures. Others might not be so obvious and are harder to measure. Some of the benefits are tangible and quantifiable, like improved project cost performance. Some are intangible, such as improved customer satisfaction, which is hard to separate from the impact of other variables.

The organizational benefits of improving project management can include these results:

- Reduced project failure costs, including cost overruns on projects and schedule delays
- Improved bottom line results for the organization as a whole
- Faster adaptability to changing circumstances
- Revenue growth
- Improved staff morale
  (Some managers may simply want to end the trauma of typical project management and to stop the bloodshed among stakeholders, team members, and managers.)
- Customer satisfaction
  (Increased customer satisfaction can be internal and external as satisfaction increases among the users of the deliverables of projects. Solid project management can also be a selling point for external customers who might see value in the use of effective processes, and who might see effective project management as a partial guarantee of product quality.)
- Reduced project management costs

- Increased productivity of project staff and staff of the organization as a whole.

It seems clear that there can be value in a project management improvement initiative. Unfortunately, that does not mean that each and every organization will achieve those benefits or achieve them at a reasonable cost.

The Challenges of Identifying the Costs and Benefits of the Investment in Project Management

Despite considerable potential benefits, it will be necessary to identify the benefits of project management for your specific organization. Identifying the actual costs and benefits of a project management initiative is not easy. Managers under pressure to provide evidence of the benefits of a project management initiative may try too hard, and the business case may deteriorate into an exercise in creative fiction.

It is usually easier to identify costs than benefits, since benefits may be more speculative than costs and may occur farther into the future than costs incurred up front. Because future benefits are hard to quantify, and because strategic benefits are particularly hard to assign dollar benefits to, some organizations have been more likely to undertake short-term projects that have immediate, measureable results than long-term, strategic projects. Though it is easier to identify a return on investment for tactical projects, it is a mistake to overlook strategic projects that may have a greater benefit in the long term.

The costs of project management improvement initiatives can include the following:

- Training and skill assessment
- The development of project management processes and tools, including processes and tools for selecting and prioritizing projects
- Investment in project management software
- Increased planning time
  (In order to reduce project risk and develop an accurate project scope, detailed project planning is required. Though the organization may "sweat the plan" and devote more resources to it than they might have earlier, they will avoid "bleeding the execution," which was often also the case earlier. In the short term, however, the costs of project planning may seem excessive to some managers who may have the propensity to demand that the project "hurry up and start delivering.")

- Recruitment costs if in-house managers are not up to the challenge of project management and must be replaced
- Staff turnover if the initiative causes some managers to leave the organization (Project management makes someone responsible for project outcomes. For those managers not comfortable with performance metrics, the organization may no longer be such a pleasant place.)
- Lost productivity, at least over the short term.
  (For a project management initiative in a functional organization, participants in the initiative may be pulled away from their "real jobs" for some time, which can create inefficiencies. Making necessary changes in organizational operations will cause some disruption and may result in the loss of short-term productivity. As indicated above, those short-term losses should be more than fully made up as the project management maturity of the organization increases.)

Unfortunately, many organizations at lower levels of project management maturity do not capture project costs. All too often, internal labor is regarded as free and not assigned to projects. Internal staff, the argument goes, would be working and being paid whether they were assigned to projects or not. If project staff are borrowed from functional organizations, they may still report their time (and their costs) to the functional organization.

> Capturing project costs is a nuisance but may be well worth the effort. Don't feel bad if your organization doesn't capture costs yet.

As a result, it is sometimes difficult to identify before and after costs of project management initiatives, and in those cases in which the organization begins to capture project costs as a part of its initiative to improve project management capabilities, new costs may seem to appear where they did not exist before. This is particularly the case with the costs of project planning, which can be considerable but are clearly worthwhile.

Measures of success for a project management initiative could include the following:

- Improved financial performance related to projects
- Improved project performance
- Enhanced organizational learning and growth
- Overall organizational success

Financial benefits of project management improvement initiatives might include improved ROI on projects, cost savings, reduction in the amount of financial capital tied up in projects, decreased cost of repeating work, decreased (over time) costs of project management, and decreased use of external resources.

Project performance improvements may include improved cost and schedule performance, increased resource utilization percentages, improved user satisfaction with project deliverables, fewer projects in process, and decreased numbers of failed projects.

Learning and growth benefits of a project management improvement initiative could include increased staff satisfaction and motivation, reduced turnover, increased organizational learning, better communications, and better ability to capture lessons learned from projects.

Ultimately, an improvement in the way an organization manages its projects should impact overall organizational success. The organization should be more flexible, more capable of meeting the needs of its customers, more efficient, more effective, and better positioned for long-term success.

Putting Together the Business Case for Project Management

The principal tool for communicating ROI and the business value of an initiative or project is the business case. The format of the business case will vary across organizations, but it will identify the problem the initiative is designed to address, the costs of the initiative, the potential benefits, and the risks. It also usually will employ some sort of evaluation tool (e.g., net present value, internal rate of return, payback) to compare the costs and the benefits.

As mentioned earlier, an effective argument for a project management improvement initiative will need to address both quantitative and qualitative evidence that the initiative will have value. It will need to include hard data and indicate that the initiative will address the organization's pain points.

The benefits of a project management initiative must be prioritized differently in each organization. In some organizations, reduced costs are very important. In others, meeting project deadlines is critical, especially if those deadlines are set externally as in the case of legally imposed requirements. Still other organizations need to vastly improve the acceptability of project results by users.

Once potential costs and benefits are identified, a technique must be applied to compare those and to determine if the initiative will produce adequate value. The best tool for this type of assessment is net present value, which is explored later in this book along with several other techniques. If the proponents of this initiative are not comfortable with the application of these analytic tools, they may need to request assistance from those who are.

> When you're done preparing the business case, put yourself in the shoes of senior managers and try to shoot it full of holes.

In some cases, the organization will establish guidelines and formats for cost and benefit estimation for the business case. Those guidelines might include the following:

- Inflation guidelines for future costs and benefits
- Types of costs and benefits to be included in the analysis
- Indirect cost rates to be applied
- Fringe benefit rates to be applied
- Required rates of return or the cost of capital, which will be discussed at length later
- The period across which the costs of capital assets will be allocated

In large organizations, it might be useful to provide project managers with training in project cost and benefit estimation so that realistic proposals can be developed.

A good business case should document these issues:

- All relevant costs
  - o Salary and benefits for internal staff as well as consultants
  - o Management time
  - o Administrative costs (secretarial time, new data needs, etc.)
  - o Training costs
  - o Vendor costs
  - o Hardware, software, and equipment
  - o Space
  - o Lost productivity
- Assumptions applied to the analysis, which should be clearly stated in the estimate of costs and benefits
  (Often, a project can be made to look favorable by the application of exaggerated assumptions.)

- Discount rates applied, if any, and the periods across which benefits will be realized
  (Special care should be taken to evaluate benefits that occur well into the future because of the difficulty in forecasting long-term benefits. If benefits are discounted to take into account the time value of money, which is discussed in Appendix 2, benefits occuring well into the future will have little impact on the net present value of the initiative.)

- Benefits that require improvements in staff efficiency or involve staff reductions
  (For example, it might be argued that the initiative will result in increased staff efficiency, but a variety of other factors outside the control of the project usually are involved in increasing staff efficiency. The assumptions behind the argument should be documented. Reductions in staff are also hard to estimate. In many cases, predicted staff savings do not occur; staff are simply reallocated to other activities. A careful evaluator of your business case will pay careful attention to these types of predicted benefits.)

- The tasks involved in the initiative and the resources necessary for them
  (The business case should identify who will be involved in each phase of the initiative and how much of their time will be required. In some cases, the resources to be employed in the initiative will be unknown at the time of the preparation of the business case. In others, resources and their costs will be known at the outset.)

- Lifecycle costing
  (Not all of the costs of the initiative will be incurred during the life of the project; others will be ongoing. Recurring benefits should be considered even if they occur beyond the life of the project; recurring costs should be considered as well.)

Rarely, a business case may have to also identify cash needs and sources. Some costs of the initiative have an immediate cash impact (e.g., equipment purchases); others don't impact the organization's cash flow (e.g., the costs of existing staff).

Creation of Organizational Commitment

The second step of the comprehensive strategy for a project management initiative is creating organizational commitment. Building that commitment can begin prior to the acceptance of the business case, but it will begin in earnest once the initiative has been approved.

Many organizations have attempted to introduce better project management discipline into their operations. Not all have been successful. One cause for failure is that too many have not built solid organizational commitment for the initiative. Without it, at the first sign of trouble or the first budget cut, the initiative is scrapped and the investment declared a waste.

The organizational commitment to improving the way projects are managed must be philosophical, economic, and organizational, and must extend from the top of the organization to the bottom. Though project management can improve organizational project management success and conserve resources in the long run, it does require an up-front investment. Staff needs to be trained, processes and methods must be developed, and tools must be purchased.

> Management buy-in isn't permanent. It takes constant attention and reinforcement.

As a result, making project management successful requires that senior managers understand the value of project management and make a commitment to it for the long term. Often, those managers will need to be convinced of the merits of a project management initiative prior to their emotional buy-in.

Even if the decision to invest in project management is made at the top of the organization, there is no guarantee that others will see the wisdom of the idea and rush to support it. Getting the buy-in of stakeholders is an ongoing process, and even though stakeholders may have expressed early buy-in, their buy-in may change over the course of the project management initiative.

Though each project management stakeholder will maintain his or her own ideas and opinions about the value of project management, some consistency of purpose and unity of thought about project management must be created. At a minimum, stakeholders should be willing to do the following:

- Commit to the experiment to improve project management
- Treat the initiative as a learning opportunity
- Support those who are on the front lines of the project management initiative
- Understand the importance of project planning
- Commit to improvement

Sometimes, however, organizations try to make the big sale for a project management initiative without having built a solid foundation for that sale. Those who are expert at solution selling know that it takes care and time to develop the trust necessary for a customer (or senior manager) to make a strategic investment. A stepwise strategy for building that trust and creating and maintaining senior level support for project management is described below.

Identify the Customers of the Initiative

One of the adages of project management is that the scope of the project must be defined if it is be successful. Part of defining the scope of the project is identifying who will be served by the project. The same thing applies to project management initiatives.

No organizational change initiative can meet the needs of every person in the organization. Though the initiative might impact everyone, it will not be able to directly meet the needs of everyone. In any project, the needs of the customer trump the needs of any other stakeholders. We can hope for a project management champion within the organization who is willing to push the initiative and guarantee the necessary funds. If that is the case, that sponsor may be the principal customer for the initative. In most cases, however, the role of champion will be shared by a variety of customers of the initiative.

Identifying the customers of the initiative allows the initiative to be targeted to their specific needs and pain points.

Build the Relationships before the Introduction of the Initiative

Why would senior managers place their trust in you to undertake an initiative to improve project management? If there is no ready answer, the first step in building support for the project management initiative is to develop trust between the proponents of that initiative and the potential customers of that initiative. Senior managers have usually learned to be skeptical of those with something to sell. Before they will even give you the time to make your pitch, they have to have developed a level of trust in you. Trust in your message will come only after trust in you.

Building that trusting relationship may take time. The best way to develop it is to build a track record of making and keeping commitments. If time is not available, trust can be earned by demonstrating relevant prior experience or exhibiting credentials. In the world of project management, certification as a Project Management Professional (PMP®) helps.

Identify the Organization's Pain Points

Despite your zeal to convince others of the value of project management, that initiative has to start with listening. Senior managers have full agendas and have to be very selective about how they invest the organization's resources and their time. To be successful at gaining their commitment, the initiative must respond to their pain points.

> Every senior manager has pain points, those things that keep them up at night. The most successful initiatives will respond to those pain points and show the promise of relief.

Pain points arise in an organization in the difference between desired states and perceptions of the actual state of affairs. For example, if investors require a rate of return on their investment in the organization that is higher than the current rate of return, a pain point is created. Similarly, a pain point will be created if managers feel that the rate of new product development is too slow or that information systems don't provide the necessary information for decision support. Managers will feel that pain as long as there is a difference between expectations and reality. Most managers spend their time attempting to minimize that pain.

Project management pain points in an organization might include the following:

- Pressure by very senior managers to deliver fast results
- Active and competent competitors
- Regulatory requirements including compliance with statutes like Sarbanes-Oxley or HIPPA
- A lack of trust in subordinate managers
- Bad experiences with prior projects
- The inability to allocate or control resources

The proponents of a project management improvement initiative should also attempt to identify opportunities to link project management improvements to other issues important to the organization. For example, a senior manager may indicate that she feels that resources are not being well managed. The project manager for the initiative could engage that manager in a discussion of how the initiative might impact resource management.

Right-Size the Initiative

Sometimes we take on more than we can accomplish and our reach exceeds our grasp. A project management initiative imposed from the top down with the intention of changing the organization in one fell swoop of training or tool application is not very likely to be successful over the long term. Clearly identifying and managing project scope are critical success factors for projects.

The size of the initiative has to be based on the size of change possible in the organization. If large-scale change is not possible immediately, small initiatives or pilot projects can develop a track record of success that can later be extended more widely.

Some care needs to be taken, however, against creating isolated silos of project management competence without a plan to spread that competence to the point at which it can develop a critical mass. Sometimes initiatives remain isolated and fail to get integrated into organizational operations. The potential for project management is lost, except for that limited local application.

Factors involved in right-sizing the initiative include the level of support for the initiative, the extent of the change required, the number of persons involved in the initiative, and the pain points addressed by the inititiave.

Provide Tangible Evidence of Success

Though we might have an emotional attachment to project management and a firmly held belief in its ability to produce results, most senior managers won't maintain long-term support of an investment without clear, measureable evidence of success. In order to provide that evidence, in the business case we need to identify the objectives of the effort and metrics for measuring progress.

For our project management initiative, we might identify such measures as the following:

- A reduction in the number of failed or challenged projects
- Reduced project budget overruns
- Improved customer or user satisfaction
- Decreased project team turnover
- Increased team member utilization as a percentage of their total time
- Reduced product defects
- Decrease in average time overrun for projects

Each of the metrics we employ has to be measureable and achievable and, most importantly, our metrics need to induce behaviors in project managers and team members that are linked to organizational goals. Once they are committed to by project managers and agreed to by stakeholders, progress against those metrics needs to be measured and reported.

Communicate in Multiple Ways

Both during the "sales" phase of the project management initiative and during its implementation, we need to communicate frequently with stakeholders. Project managers sometimes rely too extensively on the standard communication tools of project management, like standard status reports, Gantt charts, and project budget reports. Later, as we discuss the change management processes necessary to make project management successful, we learn the value of multiple means of communication with stakeholders and the value of thinking creatively about project communications.

Simply put, if we rely on standard communications in our attempt to sell project management to the organization, we may find ourselves in an endless queue of competing initiatives and fail to build the excitement we need to sustain the initiative.

Let Others Develop and Own the Solution

There is an adage that states that failure is an orphan but success has many fathers. If the project management initiative is to be successful, it must be shared by the organization.

> Harry Truman is reported to have said, "It is amazing what you can accomplish if you do not care who gets the credit." That adage is particularly true for an attempt to change an organization.

That accomplishment requires humility on the part of those intent on developing a project management initiative. It requires that they be willing to share credit for it and the responsibility for its design and implementation. With project management and other organizational initiatives, the effort can die because of a "my way or no way" attitude. The value of organizational savvy has been well-established; it is critical for successful project management initiatives.

The best managers are those who have the ability to seed ideas with others and to give away the credit for those ideas. Their reward is in the accomplishment of good results.

Expect Change

As the initiative develops, it is sure to change. No revolution, organizational or political, ever turns out the way it was intended. If we are attempting to create a revolution in the way that the organization manages projects, we have to accept the fact that the initiative will evolve over its life as well.

Change will happen in our initiative to improve project management capacity because of environmental changes, changes in personnel, changing customer needs, process changes, and technology changes. Change management is as required for this initiative as it is for any other project.

Develop a Network of Satisfied Customers and Report Success

Ultimately, the initiative will be successful and sustainable only because people in the organization see the benefits of effective project management as compared to ad hoc or traditional project management. Too often managers presume that the successes of initiatives are visible and known by all. That is not usually the case. People are busy and don't have the ability to internalize everything that goes on in the organization.

As a result successes need to be declared, and the marketing of the project management initiative needs to be continued well after the initial investment has been made. That network of satisfied customers is both a measure of the success of the initiative and a means of protecting it from an assault by the naysayers.

Simultaneous Top-Down and Bottom-Up Implementation

Top-down support is necessary for the project management initiative, but by itself, a top-down approach to project management capacity development can be resented by those at lower levels of the organization. Employees at those levels are usually adept at frustrating the initiatives of management, and without their support the initiative is likely to fail.

To balance the top-down implementation, the initiative also needs to be seeded at the bottom levels of the organization. By building skills, commitment, and excitement at the bottom of the organization, energy can be created that can sustain the initiative when senior managers fail, as they surely will, in their attempts to force project management into the organization.

> To succeed, get both those at the top of the organization and at the bottom to support the project management initiative.

Top-down strategies for project management capacity development could include the following:

- Building executive buy-in and organizational commitment
- Establishing a PMO or projectized organization

Bottom-up strategies would include the following:

- Providing project management training
- Developing a project management community of practice
- Providing tools and resources for project managers
- Establishing model projects to prove the value of project management

The combination of bottom-up and top-down implementation has a far better chance of success than an initiative supported from either the top or the bottom. Strong top-level support for the project management initiative coupled with growing competence in project management throughout the organization is a combination that is hard to defeat.

Development of Individual Competencies

Chapter 5 describes the competencies that are necessary for successful project management. Some of those competencies can be transferred to the organization by simple training programs. Others require more sophisticated methods and approaches. It is not enough that individuals develop competency in project management; the organization itself has to learn and develop the ability to continue to learn.

The Development of Project Management Processes and Procedures

One significant difference between those organizations that are at higher levels of project management maturity and those organizations at lower levels of maturity is the use of consistent project management methods. Those methods include project selection methods and prioritization methods, as well as more standard project management methods like scope definition and scheduling. Chapter 6 describes the necessary components of project management processes and methods. At the highest levels of project management maturity, the use of standardized or customized project management software is also common. The best case is that the organization develops its own project management processes and templates that are designed for its specific needs and environment.

The Creation of Organizational Structures That Support Project Management

Many organizations come to realize that they need to build organizational structures that support and foster the application of effective project management. Unfortunately, too often they turn to the most common organizational tool for project management—establishment of a project management office or PMO. PMOs can serve a useful function, though the pitfalls and problems of PMOs have not been well articulated or examined by most organizations. Chapter 8 describes organizational structures that can support an organization's effort to improve its project management capabilities.

The Creation of Project Management Communities of Practice

Most formal efforts to improve the project management capabilities of an organization eventually run out of steam. At that point, the informal mechanisms of communication and leadership that exist in every organization must take over. One informal and often overlooked mechanism for building and disseminating knowledge in an organization is a community of practice, an informal network of individuals that reaches across and through the organization to transfer information and build competence. Chapter 9 describes the operation of communities of practice and other means for project management knowledge collection, dissemination, and reuse.

Managing Organizational Change

Any project, including the initiative to increase project management capabilities across the organization, by definition creates change. If that change is not well-managed, the organizational and individual adversity to that change can frustrate the change or kill it. Project managers need to be armed with tools for dealing with change and for enlisting support for the initiative. Managing change is discussed in Chapter 10.

Summary and Conclusion

In this chapter, we described a comprehensive approach to building the project management capabilities of an organization. We also described the elements necessary for building organizational commitment to a project management initiative. The other strategies included in the comprehensive model will be described in successive chapters.

Building the project management capacity of an organization is neither simple nor easy. It requires, like all effective projects, a plan that identifies stakeholders and their needs and lays out a step-by-step solution that delivers results. It requires creativity, hard work, and constant communication. It also requires the application of the same skills, processes, and tools we will discuss later.

Table 3.1
Application of the Comprehensive Model

Component	Task
The creation of an organization-wide commitment to improve project management capability	• Identify the customers of the initiative and the metrics for success. • Build relationships early and prior to the introduction of the initiative. • Work with senior managers to create an understanding of project management and their role in supporting it, including executive training in project management as needed. • Identify and respond to management pain points with project management solutions. • Build the project management business case including identification of the required investment. • Right-size the initiative. • Provide on-going and tangible evidence of success. • Develop a communications plan for the initiative that allows for communication in multiple ways. • Let the initiative evolve and allow others to assume leadership. • Expect the initiative to change. • Build a network of satisfied customers.

Component	Task
A strategy of simultaneous top-down and bottom-up implementation	• Create a project management vision for the organization and create opportunities for senior managers to communicate the vision and endorse the initiative. • Develop and implement targeted training programs, including "hard" and "soft" skills. • Identify pilot projects for intensive application of project management. • Assist managers in applying project management tools and methods. • Measure the success of those projects against the business case. • Report results to senior managers. • Be visible; sell the initiative.
The development of individual competencies in four knowledge domains essential for project managers	• Identify training needs. • Create a training program based on the Organizational Learning Framework. • Apply project based training for key project areas. • Establish a mentoring program for ongoing learning.
The adoption of project management processes and procedures that ensure effective project management, including project selection and prioritization methods and a standard project lifecycle for similar projects	• Identify necessary standardized processes based on what the organization does at present and what it needs to attend to. • Develop, document, and install project management processes that are tailored for the organization. • Identify and apply a standard project lifecycle. • Create templates for project management. • Coach project managers in the use of the chosen project management tool. • Consider the use of an enterprise project management tool.

Component	Task
The creation of organizational structures that enhance project management, including the project management office	• Identify potential organizational structures or changes to improve project governance. • Employ project selection and prioritization processes. • Create a standard definition of the role of the project manager. • Assign and document project responsibilities. • Provide incentives for successful project management, including team incentives. • Ensure that functional managers are provided incentives for cooperation.
The establishment and nurturing of project management communities of practice and other structures that allow for ongoing organizational learning and knowledge management	• Continue to mentor project managers. • Focus on the development of intellectual capital in project management. • Create a continuity management program. • Establish a project management community of practice. • Identity learning opportunities, certification possibilities, and time available for community of practice development. • Identify those managers with the capability to serve as mentors or coaches for others.
The management and facilitation of organizational change	• Identify organizational impediments to successful project management. • Provide training to senior project managers in managing change. • Communicate with stakeholders per the communications plan for the initiative. • Create a change management plan. • Ensure organizational alignment with the goals of project management.

CHAPTER 4

Creating Effective Project Management Learning Programs

Staring down the barrel of "bet-the-organization" projects is probably not the best time to consider whether or not you have the skills in the organization to manage those projects. Nonetheless, it sometimes takes a kind of shock like the recognition of the need to pull a rabbit out of the hat to get organizations to invest in project management skill development.

In order to increase their project management capacity, organizations need to increase their human intellectual capital. Organizations can hire new staff, develop partnerships with other organizations that possess the necessary skills, or invest in the development of current staff.

In the past, organizations were faced with simple choices in the pursuit of skill enhancement for their employees. They could either build in-house human resource or training departments with the ability to create and deliver their own specific training programs, or they could open one of many readily available catalogs of courses and buy "off-the-shelf" training programs.

In an environment of constrained organizational resources and rapid change, the way that organizations are seeking to increase their internal capabilities and develop their employees is changing. Now it is not so much a matter of identifying standardized skill sets and investing in traditional instructor-led training. Because of resource constraints, organizations don't have the luxury of throwing money at training without assurance that the return on investment will be positive and fast.

Today they have options. As a result, rather than buying "off-the-shelf" courses, organizations are looking for training programs that meet their specific needs and have direct relevance to their industry or environment. Many are looking for alternative delivery methods, including E-learning, consultation, and mentoring programs. Organizations are requesting "project-based" training that allows participants to begin actual project work during the training.

These factors are reflected in the market by more careful vendor selection by buyers of training solutions, which is increasing competition, downward price pressure, and the demand for customization. Organizations are realizing that "commodity" education programs may be useful for short-term fixes, but they rarely have the capability to meet the specific and long-term needs of the organization.

This chapter explores the methods for developing the skills required for successful project management. The following chapter will identify the specific skills in these ways:

- By examining the measures for evaluating the effectiveness of training programs
- By examining the efficiency of training methods
- By identifying comprehensive, multi-dimensional strategies for enhancing skills

Later in this book, we'll examine explicit and tacit knowledge exchange. Developing project management skills, or any other skills for that matter, requires both. Explicit knowledge exchange is relatively easy; it includes standard training and learning. Tacit knowledge requires that individuals learn from one another and that the skill sets be modeled as a part of the learning experience. It takes more creativity and effort to build mechanisms for developing the tacit knowledge required for effective project management.

The Effectiveness of Training Programs

To be successful, project management training programs should be both effective and efficient; that is, they need to accomplish the objectives for which the training was applied and do it in a cost-effective manner.

To create effective outcomes, the objectives of the training must map to the business needs of the organization. In the case of the project management capacity improvement initiative, those objectives may include these measures:

- Improving project time and/or cost performance
- Improving internal and external satisfaction with project results
- Standardizing project reporting for better portfolio management and greater management visibility into projects

Note that none of these objectives is related to improving the skill levels of project managers. The ultimate measure of the effectiveness of the training program should be related to improvements in organizational performance.[3]

Surveys can be applied after training to determine the trainee's satisfaction with the training content, presentation, and environment. These assessments are easy but are not very good at measuring real outcomes. Measurement of organizational impacts is often left to chance or wishful thinking. Too often, trainers merely hope that managers will find a way to employ their new project management skills.

To make the project management initiative fully successful, the organization needs to move beyond a standard training model to a model of performance management. That movement will require identification of the organizational objectives that the program intends to achieve. A training program does not operate well in a vacuum; it is more effective for instructors and participants if the training is tied explicitly to one or more organizational goals.

Metrics for the measurement of these goals must also be identified. Not only should metrics identify success criteria for the program, they should also set upper and lower boundaries for individual participant performance before, during, and after the training. Individual performance goals should be based on common skill sets or competencies. If these competencies are based on best practice behavior, they can provide the framework of the training program itself and be integrated and coordinated in order to both build individual competencies and build organizational intellectual capital in project management.

> Though a performance management system is superior to a standard training model, few organizations will invest the time and money to create one.

Later in this chapter, we will present training options that allow for more of a performance management approach to skill development.

Training Efficiency

There is, of course, disparity in the efficiency of training programs. Unfortunately, the lowest cost options are not necessarily the most efficient. To be the most efficient, a training program or modality has to deliver the most

---

[3] The best, time-tested description of learning goals can be found in Donald Kirkpatrick, *Evaluating Training Programs: The Four Levels, 2nd Edition*. San Francisco: Berett-Koehler Publishers, 1998.

value for the lowest cost. Too often organizations invest in low cost training even though that training may have low impact on individuals or the organization. We will discuss options for training in the next section of this chapter.

The pursuit of training efficiency begins with the realization that not all staff members of the organization need the same level of training. One model for identifying training needs, the Organizational Learning Framework (OLFsm)[4] identifies four levels of competency:

- Familiarity: those persons who need to be familiar with concepts and vocabulary (e.g., team members, key stakeholders, and functional managers).

- Understanding: those persons who need to understand the concepts in more detail (e.g., project team leaders, program managers, and directly involved senior managers).

- Practice: those persons who need to apply the concepts presented (e.g., project managers).

- Coaching: those persons who need to mentor others in the concepts presented (e.g., senior project managers and project management office managers).

Project team members can benefit from an understanding of the concepts of project management, since they will be living the application of those concepts. That understanding will allow them to place activities, processes, and documents within the context of effective project management methods. Senior managers and key stakeholders should also be familiar with general concepts of project management. For them, a short, executive overview of the concepts and tools may be adequate.

Project managers need to be able to put project management concepts into practice and will require extensive skills, some of which they may already possess. The most experienced project managers can be targeted for the "coaching" level of competence so that they can lead the organizational learning effort that must occur after the formal training is complete.

If the necessary level of competence can be identified and existing skill levels assessed, training programs can be targeted to organizational needs and the amount of wasted training reduced.

---

[4] The OLF(sm) has been developed by Babbage Simmel. See www.babsim.com.

Strategies for Skill Development

In the past, skills were introduced into an organization through traditional training programs conducted either on-site or at a training center. Because customization was rare, those programs could be inexpensive and mass-produced. Unfortunately, they sometimes failed to meet the needs of individuals or organizations. Fortunately there are now a variety of innovative training methods available that can be chosen individually or combined to produce the maximum impact within the constraints of time and cost. Some of those innovative methods include the following:

- Customized curriculum, which is now possible at relatively low cost for any organization
- Project management process development as a learning experience
- Customized certification, in which the project management needs of the organization are included within a certification program requiring specific training and demonstration of competence
- E-learning, which is useful for transmitting basic project management skills and vocabulary but can fall short of building tacit knowledge
- Project-based education, which incorporates actual work and is provided to a project team, thus allowing the team to begin work on a project in the training session
- Mentoring, which provides the support of a project management professional on an as-needed basis to help project teams and/or project managers work through difficult issues or tasks on a specific project or projects

> With the training options available, no organization has to settle for programs that aren't very closely correlated with its needs.

Customized curriculum can be created at relatively low cost by starting with a base of a generic project management training program. From that point, the curriculum can be customized more extensively by creating specific curricula based on the idiosyncrasies of a company or industry. It can be updated by simply tailoring exercises and case studies. If project management methods or tools are already used in an organization, applying them in a standard project management curriculum is another customization method.

At the very least, training programs can incorporate the use of company-specific terminology, processes, or governance structures so that participants can understand project management within the context of their own organization. In addition, identification and incorporation within the training of organizational pain points can generate intense discussion which will help participants begin to apply project management concepts to their own world.

Customized curriculum provides the opportunity to focus the training on finding a solution to the organization's problems in project management rather than merely providing commodity training packages that may be off-target or irrelevant to the organization's needs.

We will explore the use of a standardized project management process as a means of developing capacity in another chapter.

Customized certification programs can be used by organizations that have developed their own project management systems and processes. Typically, a customized certification program includes targeted training in the organization's project management methodology. It may also include experience requirements and a testing component. Certification programs provide incentives for managers to become experts in the organization's project management method. Certified project managers can then be given preference in hiring, promotion, and assignment.

The key to a certification program is creating the necessary buy-in by senior managers and the project managers seeking certification. It must be seen as worthwhile, or managers will simply not put in the effort necessary for certification. Certification programs can be built from the ground up or can use existing project management models as a base. Many organizations use the Project Management Institute (PMI®) certification, the Project Management Professional (PMP®) program as their guide. PMI has created a set of standard processes as outlined in their *A Guide to the Project Management Body of Knowledge (PMBOK® Guide)—Third Edition*, which is the global standard for project management concepts. Training in project management combined with a required number of hours of experience and the successful completion of a four-hour exam make up the requirements to achieve a PMP certification. This is a strong model and can be adapted to the specific needs of an organization to ensure compliance and reliability within the organization's architecture.

Certification can also be paired with other non-traditional delivery mechanisms like e-learning. E-learning programs have proliferated in recent years and continue to grow in popularity as technology improves. E-learning can consist of readings and quizzes paired with "live" instruction" through video and/or audio connections or can take the form of web-based training which incorporates online reading and interactive quizzes and puzzles to teach the material.

E-learning is relatively inexpensive and has low unit costs, but it may not provide the richness of other training methods. It is harder to create effective dialogue between the student and the instructor over the phone or on a video conference. Students may not necessarily be focused on the material in class and instructors may have a harder time engaging them and building relationships. E-learning is best employed as part of a blended learning solution, where it can supplement instructor-led training to optimize the strengths of both training methods, or in circumstances in which face-to-face instruction is precluded by time or distance.

> E-learning programs are increasingly available and more and more sophisticated. They may be useful for meeting some training needs but may not be the best delivery mechanism for project management training unless coupled with other mechanisms.

The last two of the innovative methods, project-based training and mentoring, are explored at length below because of their ability to impart both explicit and tacit knowledge, which are both required for increasing the intellectual capital of the organization.

Project-Based Education

Traditional, instructor-led project management training is usually indifferent to the type of projects the attendees manage. In the best case, standard training packages can be modified to better fit the needs of the organization, or case studies specific to the circumstances of an organization can be created if managers from the same organization are being trained. Traditional, instructor-led training assumes that participants in the training will internalize the concepts being presented and find their own ways to apply those concepts in their own workplace. That assumption is not always valid. For it to be true, participants in the training need to comprehend and internalize the concepts, they have to be motivated to apply the concepts they've been exposed to, and the organization has to be configured to allow their new skills to be applied.

As an alternative, project-based education brings the organization and its own projects to the training. It uses real projects and trains either the project team as a whole or managers from across the organization. The curriculum is designed to address the real problems the organization faces. Instead of assuming that managers will make use of the concepts they have been exposed to, project-based training requires them to apply those concepts to real projects before they leave the program. By the close of a project-based training program, managers will have begun the planning process for current projects and will have developed templates for further project planning and management.

Project-based education allows students to apply new skills immediately to problems that are real. It creates a safe setting for the project team or management team to begin the dialogue necessary to resolve conflict and create innovation. In addition, students can leave the training session with completed deliverables for their projects.

Project-based training may be a little more expensive than traditional project management training, but it has the potential for faster development of project management capabilities and greater retention of concepts.

One way to jump start the development of project management capabilites is to create a demonstration project that is managed well. Nothing sells project management in an organization better than success. Project-based training can not only increase skills but also set up a project for success.

> Project-based training quickly links project management concepts to the reality of the organization.

Examples of specific areas that could be addressed in a project-based workshop include the following:

- Scope planning
- Creation of the work breakdown structure and activity lists
- Construction and analysis of project network diagrams
- Project risk identification and risk response identification
- Managing project costs if requested
- Project communications planning

These areas are critical for successful project management and have the potential for creating useful dialogue, which the instructor must be able and willing to facilitate.

Mentoring

More traditional training programs can be employed to acquire some of the necessary project management skills in areas such as application of project management tools, process diagramming, scheduling, and the other "hard" project management disciplines. But as organizations adapt to meet the needs of a challenging environment, they are discovering that their efforts to introduce new skills and competencies into the organization may not be producing the results they expect or require.

Though investment in disciplines like project management can provide new tools and techniques, organizations report that fundamental changes in organizational performance often do not follow. Those types of changes require more fundamental, individually based skill development than can be produced by standard training and learning methods. Deep and sustainable organizational change requires one-on-one mentoring of those who must *become* the change the organization requires.

Increasingly, it is also becoming apparent that the adoption of hard skills, even within targeted project management disciplines, is inadequate to ensure organization success, the effective implementation of project management initiatives, or skill transfer necessary to sustain the initiative. Implicit in the effective adoption of project management are the development and application of certain soft skills, including the following:

- Making things happen within the specific constraints of an organization
- Interpersonal communications
- Managing conflict within the team and among stakeholders
- Knowledge management and continuity management
- Managing change
- Building and maintaining buy-in
- Marketing the project
- Leadership

Though training programs can help develop the foundations for the development of these skills, their application often requires individual interaction and expert knowledge of the specific organizational situation in which these skills must be applied. Effective application often requires one-on-one dialogue, personally focused development, and progressive skill application.

Mentoring programs for managers and project teams can improve individual skills, enhance the adaptability of the organization, and reduce the time it takes to adopt effective change in the way that projects are managed. A mentoring program can be structured to provide one-on-one assistance to project managers or to provide assistance to the project team.

Mentoring is based on the following premises:

- Effective change requires the adoption of soft skills as well as the development of hard skills in necessary disciplines.
- Sustainable organizational change will not result without both.

- The transfer of soft skills requires a different set of education delivery mechanisms than hard skills.
- Soft skill transfer and development require individual attention and knowledge of the specific needs of the organization and the circumstances of the individual.

Managers and leaders often need an external influence in order to change perspectives, recognize necessary aptitudes, frame action agendas, craft action agendas, and evaluate their actions. Mentoring within a carefully crafted program can provide a mechanism for skill improvement, knowledge transfer both within and across employee generations, productivity enhancement, ROI generation, and leadership development. Mentoring can become a springboard to improvement of morale and increased retention of key staff. In addition, mentoring can also break down organizational silos by enhancing trust throughout the organization.

The primary focus of a mentoring program is the enhancement of individual skills, which will be enhanced through both being mentored and being a mentor. Mentoring can provide a renewed sense of purpose to mentors, who will likely value the opportunity to transfer their wisdom to others. As individual skills are improved, organizational productivity and the ability of the organization to successfully change will also be enhanced.

> Even the most accomplished project managers can benefit from mentoring.

Mentoring is different from coaching. Coaching is performed by the supervisor and operates within the constraints of the organization's hierarchy. Mentoring is performed by an assigned mentor who is normally outside the management reporting structure of the client (the person being mentored). Therefore, mentoring has the potential to build relationships that transcend the organizational hierarchy. Mentors from outside the organization can draw on their experience and expertise and bring new skills and perspectives into the body of knowledge of the organization.

Though the mentoring program must be tailored to the unique needs of the organization, a project management mentoring program should contain the following key elements:

- Expression of organizational support for the mentoring program
- Identification of the focus of the program
- A mentoring training program

- Assignment of trained mentors for a fixed period of time
- A clear understanding of the program by both the mentor and the client
- A clearly defined set of expectations for the mentor

Expression of Organizational Support for the Mentoring Program

This support may include a statement by management, participation by senior managers, and the establishment of support mechanisms. These mechanisms might include the provision of time for mentors and clients to meet, resource materials, or incorporation of mentoring duties into job descriptions or performance expectations.

Identification of the Focus of the Program

Not all mentoring programs have the same purposes. Some are designed to improve project management skills. Others might be designed to develop future leaders. Still others might be designed to transfer knowledge across employee generations. No matter what the focus, that focus should heavily influence the design of the program.

A Mentoring Training Program

Not all people have the requisite skills for effective mentoring. Mentors may need to be trained on their role and the skills necessary for effective mentoring. They must meet professional requirements, agree to a set of standards for the program, and be assigned from outside the chain of command of the person to be mentored. This last provision ensures that the mentoring relationship is focused on personal and organizational growth rather than on daily assignments and accountability. Often the mentor will be older than the client, though all persons of any age or at any level of the organization can benefit from mentoring. As a signal of the importance of the program, senior managers may also choose to be assigned a mentor.

A Clear Understanding of the Program by Both the Mentor and the Client

Both the mentor and the client need to understand the limits and attributes of the program. An agreement between the mentor and client should be discussed and signed by both. Both will be required to adhere to standards of professional conduct.

A Clearly Defined Set of Expectations for the Mentor

In a project management mentoring situation, mentors can help the client apply project management tools and methods to specific projects, adapt to project change, frame effective strategies for project success, and make better decisions about the project. The mentor can provide support and guidance that help the client resolve both personal and organizational conflict. The mentor functions as a trusted advisor who is focused more on helping the client make the right decisions than on providing specific task-based direction. The outcome should be a relationship that allows both the mentor and the client to grow personally and professionally.

An important function of the mentor is to provide an ear or sounding board for the client. Effective listening also demonstrates that the mentor has empathy for the needs of the client. Empathy is also required if trust is to be established. Without that trust, the mentor-client relationship will fail to produce effective outcomes.

With an understanding of the client situation, the mentor can honestly provide perspective and a framework for assisting the client in making decisions.

The mentor can also challenge the client to improve his or her skills or respond to the challenges they face.

In an effective mentoring relationship, the mentor *cannot* act as a substitute for or undermine the existing management structure. He or she should not encourage behavior that is harmful to the organization nor engage in unprofessional behavior with regard to the client. Lastly, and perhaps most important, the mentor should never violate the confidence of the client. This will undermine the basis of trust on which the mentor-client relationship is built and will make it difficult for the client to accept further assistance.

Mentoring programs can be effective across a wide array of disciplines, including project management. If they are successful, they will generate an energy of their own that can help sustain the project management initiative over time.

Summary and Conclusions

The creation and transfer of knowledge across the organization require that the organization identify who to train and what skills they need most. Broad-based programs that don't pinpoint necessary skill sets and the level of learning required run the risk of over-training some while failing to meet the needs of others.

A variety of innovative forms of learning are available as alternatives to traditional, instructor-led training using standard curricula. Among those alternative methods are project based education and mentoring.

Both methods allow for the enhancement of individual and team skills and effective knowledge transfer across the organization and across employee generations. They help the organization both learn and apply project management techniques.

Successful training programs need to increase individual skill levels, increase the project management maturity of the organization, and improve the organization's ability to continuously learn. Ultimately, their success must be measured against the organization's ability to manage projects within the unique constraints and environmental context of the organization.

Jump-Starting the Project Initiative
Creating Effective Learning Programs

- Interview a few managers to determine the level of project management knowledge held by project managers and team members.
- Identify the funds available for training.
- Survey the training options available (on-line, instructor led, etc.).
- Build a comprehensive training program making use of as many mechanisms for knowledge transfer as possible.
- Leverage your training budget by employing mentoring programs or using in-house instructors.
- Whenever possible, make use of customized curriculum so that it is relevant to managers and team members.
- Frequently evaluate your training programs.
- Strive to build the capacity of the organization to educate itself in order to create self-sustaining learning.

Case Study in Organizational Learning in Project Management: Project-Based Training and Mentoring

A state agency saw the need to revise its operations to better serve its clients and interface with federal agencies that are sources of its funding. It correctly defined the necessary change as a multi-dimensional set of projects within a broader program of system-wide change. The agency realized that those projects would require complex interactions among internal and external stakeholders, including federal officials and state legislators, and deliverables that had to meet state and federal standards. The agency also realized that these projects were a key to the effectiveness of the organization and that it did not have the skills in project management that would be required to deliver these projects successfully. The challenge was daunting.

Initially, the agency attempted to purchase training for its managers in the use of a project management tool. Ultimately, the agency elected to adopt the more comprehensive approach.

The program began with three one-day project management workshops: project management fundamentals, an application workshop, and a workshop on the use of the project management tool. The program also included mentoring for the project team that could be requested at will.

The first workshop brought together the major stakeholders for the project, including the project managers and key team members. It was customized with case studies relevant to the organization. The second workshop was attended by project managers and key team members. In that workshop, templates were provided for project planning and the facilitators coached the participants through the development of elements of the project plan. The tool workshop allowed the project team to load its own project data into the tool.

Two mentoring sessions were arranged for the project team. The first brought together the project manager and a key stakeholder to refine and reach agreement on the scope of the project. The second mentoring session helped design a communications plan for the project.

As a result, in a very short time the organization was able to introduce new skills, make immediate use of those skills, apply a standard project management tool, develop confidence in its ability to manage critical projects that had seemed overwhelming, and work through the rough spots of application with the help of the mentors. The organization was very satisfied with the program and felt that they had gained real value for their investment.

CHAPTER 5

The Necessary Skills for Effective Project Management

There are some people who are natural project managers and just have a knack for getting things done. They make project management look easy. For most of us, however, managing projects is a challenge that calls on many different skills and abilities and often a healthy dose of luck.

After identifying the best methods for skill development, as discussed in the last chapter, the next step for organizations is to determine which skill sets its managers must acquire. Some of those skill sets are familiar. Some are ancillary to project management. Some are easy to learn, and some are complex and hard to master.

One of the most significant challenges of project management is the breadth of the skills required, and it is a wonder that any single project manager can master them adequately. Project managers must be able to effectively utilize hard skills like building project network diagrams, identifying the critical path and compressing the schedule, applying quality control techniques, analyzing risk, understanding the technology of the chosen solution, and applying cost estimating and control techniques. They must also be able to incorporate use of soft skills such as managing stakeholder expectations, communicating effectively with a wide array of internal and external stakeholders, managing and resolving conflict, and conducting successful negotiations.

If project managers do not have the skills that match the considerable challenges they will face, they will not only fail to be successful but can become frustrated, stressed out, and even burned out.

In this chapter, we'll examine four domains of project management competency. Each of those domains will be explored, and the challenges of each will be identified. Last, we'll examine the skills that can enhance the ability of an individual to manage projects, including the necessary soft skills and a set of ancillary skills related to project management, which support the project management process.

The Four Domains of Project Management

How do we choose project managers? Do we assign them to projects based on their knowledge of the technology, their communications skills, their project management experience, or their availability?

Despite the fact that the selection of a project manager for a key project can make the difference between success and failure, organizations have few models that can help define the skills most appropriate to a specific project. With the model described below, four domains of project management are identified that can help make decisions about whom to assign as the project manager and which skills to target for improvement. In addition, this model can be applied to develop a project team that complements the skills of the project manager.

All too often, it is assumed that projects are managed best by those who are subject matter experts (SMEs), usually in the technology used to solve the problem that generated the project. Most vividly, information technology projects are nearly always managed by those with expertise in the software solution, which has advantages and disadvantages that will be discussed later.

> Expertise on the solution used to address the problem the project has been designed to solve, though important, is over-rated.

Instead of focusing on just subject matter knowledge, project managers need to master four interrelated knowledge domains. These are the domains:

- Knowledge of the solution
- Knowledge of the problem
- Knowledge of the process
- Knowledge of the context

Those four domains interact as illustrated in the following diagram. Each is discussed in turn.

The Knowledge Domains for Successful Project Management

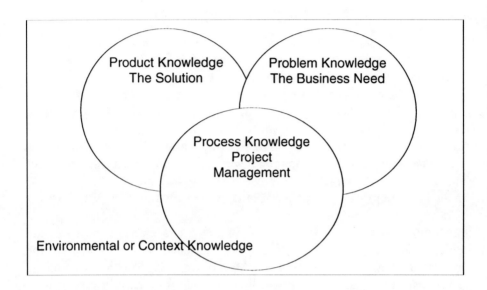

The Product Knowledge Domain

Do project managers need to be subject matter experts (SMEs)? Most of those who assign project managers would argue that they do. Many organizations feel that project managers must understand in some detail the solution to the problem. They should understand the configuration and implementation requirements for the product that the project is intended to produce.

As a result, project managers are most often assigned from engineering or other technology disciplines. Engineers manage construction projects, and information technology professionals manage most projects with an IT solution to the problem the project was designed to address, regardless of the business need.

Some knowledge of the product of the project is imperative. But is it the most critical skill set for successful project managers? Those who argue that product knowledge is the most critical skill set maintain that only with a full and complete understanding of the product can a project manager solve project problems. They believe that unless the project manager is the SME, the project team cannot be effectively managed, and project problems and risks cannot be fully comprehended. SMEs, it is argued, have the ability to make judgments about solution alternatives and the ability to optimize the application of the technology.

Too often, however, project managers are assigned simply because they are the most competent SME. In some cases, the skills necessary for being an SME are not the same skills that make good project managers. Too often SMEs haven't developed good communications skills, the ability to delegate, the skills or understanding necessary for managing the conflicts inherent in projects, or the ability to manage the sophisticated relationships inherent in complex projects.

If the project manager is an SME, he or she may exhibit tunnel vision with regard to the solution being considered and may not have the ability to fairly evaluate a full range of solution alternatives. Too often they focus on the technical aspects of the project and overlook the needs for stakeholder communications and the business purpose for which the project was initiated.

Project managers who have a strong command of the product domain are challenged to take these steps:

- Consider a range of solutions and recognize the shortcomings of the solution
- Communicate effectively with non-technical staff
- Allow other project staff to have a voice in the project
- Delegate the performance of critical activities
- Focus on solving business problems

Too often, a product focus causes project managers to fail to consider a broad range of solutions. They may not recognize the complexity of the organizational issues and fail to include all of the impacted stakeholders in the development of requirements and the project plan.

The Problem Knowledge Domain

Project managers with a strong focus in the problem knowledge domain are experts in business processes and practices. Accountants can be assigned as project managers for building and installing accounting systems; lawyers manage legal projects; and business managers are assigned to improve business processes. Problem knowledge requires understanding of the business problem to be addressed by the project. It requires a focus on what problem the project has been initiated to solve.

Project managers with knowledge of the business have an advantage in defining the project scope or requirements. Their projects are more likely than others to meet customer demands and create deliverables that conform to user requirements and are fit for their use.

> Since most of our project failures are caused by the failure of the project to meet user needs, wouldn't it make sense to employ business area experts as project managers instead of SMEs?

Though they may be able to effectively communicate with business users, problem experts may be less able to communicate with the project team. They may have less knowledge of the solution than team members and may be at the mercy of SMEs. On the other hand, they may be able to ask key questions of SMEs that can keep the project focused on meeting the needs for which it was initiated.

The challenges for project managers who are most skilled in the problem domain will be to do the following:

- Communicate with technical experts
- Understand the limits and possibilities of the selected solution or potential solutions
- Ask questions of SMEs that will keep the solution in perspective as a tool for solving the business problem

The Process Knowledge Domain

The creation of a project management profession has created a class of managers who are able to organize projects and apply tools and techniques to the management of projects of all varieties. The tools and techniques of project management articulated by organizations like the Project Management Institute are indifferent to the type of project they are applied to.

Does that mean that a manager schooled in professional project management can manage any type of project without an understanding of the problem or the solution? Probably not, but the application of project management processes can certainly improve any project. Project managers armed with that knowledge can establish orderly and comprehensive processes, document the assumptions, provide an agreed-upon project plan, and build communications mechanisms that keep stakeholders involved and satisfied. Even without a detailed understanding of either the solution or the problem, a project manager with the ability to apply project management processes can accomplish these goals:

- Ensure stakeholder agreement on the scope of the project
- Facilitate the development of a project plan
- Communicate with stakeholders
- Analyze and manage project risk
- Organize the project through the creation of a work breakdown structure
- Apply cost and time management techniques

A project manager whose principal skills are related to the processes and tools of project management must meet these challenges:

- Developing an understanding of the business problem and the proposed solution
- Tailoring project management methods for the situation
- Facilitating interactions between SMEs and the business users of the product of the project

The Context Knowledge Domain

Underlying the knowledge domains discussed thus far is the management of the environment of the project or context knowledge. Context-focused project managers work at managing the context within which the project operates and managing the relationships among stakeholders. It requires some understanding of all three other knowledge domains.

Context management is particularly important for complex projects with multiple stakeholders. It doesn't require detailed knowledge of the technology employed but is more concerned with relationship management and communications. Context management is also ideal for management of projects employing vendors because of the information asymmetry that usually characterizes vendor relationships.

Context managers focus on the *how* of decisions rather than the *what*. When a problem arises, they gather information about the problem, attempt to identify objective decision criteria, approach decision making as a collaborative learning experience for themselves and the team, and measure the results and evaluate the decision. Context managers are principally externally focused; they focus on building relationships, delegate effectively, tolerate ambiguity and differences of opinion, build team capability, and use conflict and mistakes as learning opportunities

> Context managers focus more on how the team responds to problems rather than the details of the solution.

Context management requires skills in these fields:

- Communications
- Conflict management
- Stakeholder assessment and relationship building
- Marketing
- Organizational politics
- Motivation

Properly applied, context management ensures full involvement of stakeholders and provides good communications.

Context-focused project managers will meet these challenges:

- Adequately understanding the technology in the project
- Identifying important project details
- Delegating effectively when they may not fully understand the task
- Controlling through accountability for outcomes
- Creating and managing good boundaries
- Protecting the project team from the remainder of the organization

Blending the Knowledge Domains

It is obvious that an understanding of all four knowledge domains is necessary for effective project management. Unfortunately, too little time is usually spent developing skills in the environmental or context domain. Though training abounds in the tools of project management, more attention must be given to soft skill development, which is essential to the management of complex projects but is more difficult to master for many project managers.

> If the project manager isn't strong across the four knowledge domains, the project team should include those who can complement his or her ability.

We can also employ the model described above to create a comprehensive project team. For example, if we can identify a strong technology leader and employ solid business and systems analysts, we could then assign a project manager to manage the context and the project management process. A more detailed description of the roles and functions of systems and business analysts will be discussed later in this chapter.

It can be argued that the best (and most highly paid) project managers have highly developed environmental and soft skills. Those are the project managers who can manage change in addition to implementing new processes and systems.

The Necessary Skills for Project Managers

To improve its ability to consistently deliver successful projects, an organization needs to acquire certain skill sets, either by hiring project managers who possess those skills or by introducing those skills to current staff through standard or tailored training programs. In this section, we'll examine the range of skills necessary for effective project management.

The PMI® Role Delineation Study

The best assessment of the skills necessary for project management has been conducted by the Project Management Institute (PMI®) in its *Role Delineation Study*. That study, which was begun in 1999, employed a panel of experts to delineate the field of project management. The results of the study were validated by a survey of project managers, and specifications for project manager certification were identified.

The Role Delineation Study identified six performance domains for project managers that paralleled the process groups identified by the *PMBOK® Guide* (initiating, planning, executing, controlling, and closing) with the addition of professional responsibility. Across those six performance domains, the study identified forty-five tasks and listed the knowledge and skills each required of project managers.

The skill sets identified by the study can be categorized as hard project management skills or soft skills, though the names applied to the categories do not properly identify their importance or difficulty and may not be entirely exclusive. The hard skills for project management are those that are related to the application of project management tools, processes, or methods. They include these skills:

- Gathering, assessing, and integrating information
- Using selected tools
- Developing time cost and resource estimates and schedules
- Using project performance management tools
- Administering contracts
- Organizing and documenting information

> Too many project managers have strong hard-skill competency but inadequate soft skills.

The surprising finding of that study is the preeminence of what are sometimes referred to as *soft skills*. Those soft skills are related to the ability of the project manager to interact with people, motivate the team, and sell the project to stakeholders. The most often cited skill is communicating effectively. The second most common skill set necessary for project management involves negotiating or conflict management. The *Role Delineation Study* identified these soft skills as being necessary for project management:

- Communicating effectively
- Negotiation and conflict management
- Facilitating meetings and presenting information
- Writing effectively and persuasively
- Exercising self-control
- Maintaining an open mind
- Embracing diversity
- Exercising tolerance and compromise
- Exhibiting empathy

Many project managers excel at one or the other type of skills, but few excel at both. Many project managers are adept at the hard side of project management, which is natural given that many project managers have roots in the technology being applied. It is rarer to find a project manager able to apply the soft skills, but without them adverse project consequences will likely result. If single individuals cannot be identified with a fully rounded skill set, it may be possible to construct a project team that provides a balance of skills.

Soft Skills for Project Managers

The soft skills for project management are often the most difficult to transfer but often are the difference between average project managers and excellent ones. Unfortunately, the abilities to communicate, empathize, listen, and facilitate are often influenced by a variety of factors, including personality type and culture, and take specialized training and time to master. These skills are hard to transfer by traditional learning programs. Instead, they require a blend of training, application/practice, and mentoring.

As noted earlier, communicating effectively is probably the most important skill of project managers. Communications can be categorized as gathering information (input), disseminating information (output), and creating effective dialogue (a blend of the two). Each requires a different skill set. Gathering information requires that the project manager have the ability to listen actively, confirm that his or her understanding is correct, and reframe what people have said into useful information.

Disseminating information employs skill sets that many of us are familiar with, like making presentations, which will be discussed below. Creating a dialogue requires the ability to allow people to engage in open information sharing in a non-threatening environment in which they are able and willing to open themselves to the interests of the other parties. Dialogue is very valuable for project team activities such as building a work breakdown structure or identifying risk.

> Every project manager must be able to facilitate effective dialogue. If they can't, they'll either become too directorial or simply not gather the valuable perspectives of stakeholders.

Effective communication requires the ability to choose communication methods, and project managers need to be able to listen effectively. Listening is an active endeavor; we can't listen while we check e-mail, stare out the window, or think about something else. Listening effectively requires that the project manager control the pace and the direction of the conversation by asking questions that bring the speaker back on point and clarify key points. It is important that the project manager recognize the emotion in the speaker's story, but in most instances, it is necessary for the listener to reframe the comments into useful information.

Reframing is a technique for restating what the speaker has said in more neutral or positive terms. It requires practice but can be effectively applied to reduce and understand conflict. While the listener needs to be actively engaged, the listener also needs to fight the urge to make assumptions or make decisions too early. Periodically throughout the conversation, the project manager needs to ensure that he/she fully understands the story and make the speaker aware that they understand.

Making effective presentations is one of the most critical skills required of project managers. Although many project managers are uncomfortable with making presentations, everyone can improve their skills with coaching and practice. Effective presentations require a match between the needs of the audience, the type of presentation, and presentation style.

Meetings are a staple of projects, but effective meetings don't happen by accident. They take management by the facilitator before, during and after the meeting. Project meetings are held for a variety of purposes, including disseminating information, generating input, and developing the team. The most important role of the meeting facilitator is to ensure that all communications are understood, are on target for the purpose of the meeting, and are productive. That requires active listening and management of the dialogue through targeted questions, reframing, and summarization. Each comment by participants should be analyzed and linked back to the purpose of the meeting.

In addition to well-developed communication skills, both verbal and written, the project manager must be able to serve in a leadership role representing the business user goals for the project or process. Exercising leadership in an organization or project doesn't require formal, assigned authority. In fact, new leadership models emphasize distributed leadership and emergent leadership. Those models argue that the most important leadership roles in a project are not usually filled by those who are provided leadership titles or formal roles.

Influencing the organization is that vital function of being able to get things done within the organization. It is sometimes described as *organizational savvy*. It takes an understanding of human motivations and an understanding of the organization, which sometimes can only be learned over time.

Last, the project manager has to be able to build and sustain relationships. Relationship building within the project environment takes many of the same skills as exercising leadership and influencing the organization. It is the process of building trust among stakeholders that allows for effective communications and action.

Ancillary Skill Sets for Project Teams

As difficult as it is to develop both hard and soft skills specific to project management, those skills are usually not adequate to allow organizations to consistently deliver project results. Other skill sets are necessary to allow the organization to leverage and support effective project management.

It is unlikely that the project manager will possess all of the skills described above. As a result, care must be taken to assemble a project team that is fluent in project management terminology and basic project management concepts but can also provide ancillary support to the project manager in key areas. In addition, the project manager must understand the importance of these ancillary skill sets and ensure that these key functions are performed, and that the team has the opportunity to develop its capabilities.

> Someone on the project team must have the responsibility for identifying and documenting the needs of the ultimate user of the product of the project.

In some projects, the project manager will be required to perform all of the ancillary functions listed below. In a more mature project management environment, roles would be delineated and assigned to those with the best skills for the specific function.

These are ancillary skill sets that can enhance the ability of the project team to function and deliver project results:

- Requirements definition and documentation
- Business analysis
- Systems analysis
- Process improvement

Each of these ancillary skill sets is described below.

Requirements Definition and Documentation

There is no more critical function in the management of successful projects than identifying a clear project scope, which includes identifying the requirements of the product the project will create. Requirements include both the business requirements and the system or technical requirements.

Unfortunately, identifying these requirements is difficult under the best circumstances. Often requirements are poorly understood even by business users of the systems or products to be created by the project. Users often have a difficult time articulating those requirements, and frequently the requirements will change during the course of the project. Those who develop the product of the project may also bring their own biases to product design, which may further complicate the ability of the project to produce deliverables that meet user needs.

In order to accurately define and document user requirements, the project team must be able to identify the "must have" requirements and the "nice to have" requirements by fully understanding what the user needs. This requires some knowledge of the user's business processes since they will need to map the business process as it is now (the "as is" process) and how they would like to work as a result of the project (the "to be" process). Process flows and other workflow diagrams can later be documented to serve as the baseline for what is in scope and what is out.

It is critically important that a clear scope definition be created, and substantial time should be dedicated to creating a clear consensus on customer needs and a product design that meets the user's needs. Scope management processes are designed to develop a clear understanding of the project requirements, document those requirements, and manage changes that will arise during the course of the project.

To deliver successful projects, the project team needs to build on the scope management processes within the *PMBOK® Guide* to create an effective requirements gathering process and a system for managing requirements changes.

There are several commonly used types of requirements documentation including general business requirements, functional specifications (generally used for software implementation), use cases (used for object-oriented software projects) and technical specifications (or design documents). Each of these provides more detail about the needs of the user.

In order to elicit this level of detail, project team members or the project manager must call upon some of the communication, negotiation, and listening skills covered earlier. One or more of the project team members must conduct effective one-on-one interviews and/or shadow the appropriate users to make sure that common and exception processes are captured. The team should also maintain a log of common terminology that specifies exactly what a certain process, time requirement, or exception means. This will decrease the probability that the end product of the project will not meet user expectations.

Without good requirements definition, we tend to make incorrect assumptions, fail to identify all of the requirements for project success, develop inconsistent definitions of requirements, and let each stakeholder develop his or her own definition of the requirements, which will ultimately lead to dissatisfaction. The project team and/or project manager must manage user/stakeholder expectations by clearly and consistently communicating with those stakeholders.

One of the hardest parts of requirements gathering in a project is the fact that business and priorities change so quickly that requirements that once made sense may no longer work as the project progresses. In order to maintain control of the product but still ensure that it meets user/stakeholder goals, the project manager must employ a requirements change control process by which new requirements are reviewed, estimated, and approved or denied for inclusion. The transparency of this process is critical to maintaining the support and understanding of users/stakeholders and the sponsors. Again, this process requires clear and constant communication to ensure that the full team has been apprised of each change to the project scope.

Business Analysis

Business analysts serve as the link between the business interests served by the project and the technology that will be employed to deliver the functionality required by it. They are responsible for translating business needs into language that systems analysts can turn into a solution, for framing the problem, and identifying the most appropriate solution. They keep the project focused on the needs for which it was initiated. They are often charged with gathering documenting and testing requirements, especially in software development and implementation projects.

The business analyst must understand both the business process and the technology that enables that process. Understanding these business drivers will help business analysts to put the project in the appropriate context.

In additional, articulation of the "pain points" associated with the current business process is essential to appropriately applying technology. The phrase "paving the cow path" is often used to describe automation projects that do not address the root cause of a particular business problem.

Root cause analysis is one tool that helps business analysts fully understand the scope of the problem that spawned the project. Once they understand the problem, they can then offer alternative solutions—either process changes, system changes, or both. This helps to define the scope of the project and is reinforced by the boundaries set by the initial process analysis. Root cause analysis can also help to identify additional stakeholder groups and cross project impacts.

Once the problem has been identified, business analysts can go about the requirements gathering and documentation process more effectively. They can also begin conversations with solution developers and other technical personnel to ensure that the alternative solutions make sense within the bounds of the project constraints.

As the project continues, the business analyst also applies his or her knowledge of the process and the new system to develop test scripts, acceptance criteria, and training materials. They are an extension of the user/stakeholder community and therefore act on their behalf on a project team. The business analyst is the voice of the user in technical meetings and in testing.

Systems Analysis

On software development and implementation projects, systems analysts work to further translate the business need into the technological solution. They develop the detailed design that enables the product or service to be created. Systems analysts, or architects, create and document various models that provide the foundation of a system design. They may start with a logical design that identifies how the system works conceptually. This logical design is used to create increasingly detailed designs that are ultimately used to code the system itself. Together with the business analyst, they create an end-to-end project solution that meets user needs in the most efficient and effective manner.

The solution development team's primary project team function is to design and plan the project outcomes. They focus on using the business requirements (i.e., the *what* of the project) in the context of the business need (i.e., the *why* of the project) in order to accurately devise the methods and tools to use to reach the solution (i.e., the *how* of the project).

> Whether your project is building a bridge, assessing training needs, or building an information system, someone has to translate the user's needs into language the solution creator can understand.

Necessary skills for systems analysis include the following:

- Understanding of the technology to be applied to solve the business problem
- Developing solutions employing the technology of the project
- Communicating with technical staff and the business analyst
- Documenting the solution/system
- Developing process and system testing

Process Improvement

Very often, at the heart of a project is the need to improve processes. In fact, any attempt to improve organizational processes can be defined as a project because it has a limited duration and provides unique product, service, or result.

Other organizations have created a management architecture driven by projects Examples are law and accounting firms and consulting and construction organizations.

> The best information technology projects make sure that they don't simply automate ineffective processes.

Process improvement and project management are complementary skills. Sometimes the project manager is chosen for his or her expertise in process improvement. These process improvement tools help a project manager effectively manage:

- Process mapping
- Workflow diagramming
- Cause and effect diagramming
- Root cause analysis
- Gap analysis
- Statistical analysis
- Quality control techniques

Incorporation of effective business and systems analysis and automation tools, sometimes referred to as business process management (BPM), is becoming a focus of those involved in the creation of business value. BPM tools, which can include such concepts as end-to-end process analysis, can be linked with effective project management to improve ROI and help organizations close the gap between their current reality and their aspirations.

Summary and Conclusions

Given the sizeable range of required skills, it is a wonder that successful project managers can be found or developed. Project management requires knowledge across the four knowledge domains described in this chapter— hard project skills, soft skills, and several ancillary skills. Other chapters described methods for building those skills and assessing where the most work needs to be done.

It may be the case that project managers in your organization do not possess adequate skills in each of the areas listed above. In that case, care needs to be taken to build a project team with a combination of individual talents that covers all the bases.

CHAPTER 6

Development of Standardized Project Management Processes

Critical to building project management capability that extends throughout the organization is the development of a standard project management methodology. Without a standard methodology, each project manager or organizational unit will have an incentive to build their own method, which will limit the ability of the organization to share resources, identify project status, and manage a project portfolio.

A project management methodology that is standardized across the organization allows for these points:

- Common understanding of project status since the same terms will be applied to all projects and status metrics will have been developed

- Greater flexibility in the assignment of resources since team members and managers will all understand the process and be able to speak the same language

- Clear expectations for project managers, which should be articulated by the methodology
  (New project managers can be "handed the manual" that describes how the organization manages its projects and what the expectations are of project managers.)

- Standard documents that should allow managers to compare projects and not waste time interpreting different formats and reports

- Faster project start-up time because the steps in project start-up will be documented

- Better ability to share lessons learned given a standard, repeatable process and common vocabulary

There are a variety of project management methods available. In order to maximize its effectiveness, a standardized project management methodology should contain these items:

- Documents and procedures for project initiation and selection
- Templates for project planning
- A step-wise process to be followed for all projects
- Elective elements that can be applied dependent on project needs
- Clear articulation of the purpose and intended outcomes of each project management process
- Identification of the persons responsible for the project and articulation of project roles
- Opportunities for communication of lessons learned
- Analytic methods for project tracking and performance management

A project methodology can be developed from the ground up or can use existing templates and methods. The preeminent project management standard has, of course, been developed by PMI and is detailed in the *PMBOK® Guide*. Some would also argue that the *PMBOK® Guide* also presents a project management methodology by defining and describing project management processes. Basing the project management methodology of the organization on the *PMBOK® Guide* ensures that the method employed is thorough and meets international standards for project management excellence. Employing a project management methodology that is consistent with the *PMBOK® Guide* makes communication with vendors and external resources easier and ensures that those external resources can quickly and easily understand and implement your project management methods.

Building a customized methodology for the organization also has benefits. A customized methodology can include specialized tools and processes that are particularly relevant to the organization. It can address the relative level of project management sophistication of the organization's managers and the organization's need for project documentation.

This chapter describes the standard processes that an organization's project management methodology should contain. Whether or not the organization creates a formal, mandatory method or less formal methods, it should include processes to accomplish the following functions:

- Project selection
- Project initiation

- Identification of the project's scope, which includes
  o Scope planning
  o Requirements definition
  o Work breakdown structure development and activity definition
- Risk planning and tracking
- Resource planning and management
- Cost planning and tracking
- Effective communications
- Performance reporting
- Project change control
- Project closure

Each of these functions is explained and the value of each described in the remainder of this chapter.

Project Selection

All too often, organizations have no clearly defined rules for creating projects. As a result, projects pop up everywhere. It is not uncommon for organizations to be able to identify dozens if not hundreds of current projects, some that have unknown origins, some with no apparent end, and some that are very important to the organization. Without project selection and prioritization methods, project priorities are assigned by the individual project manager, if there is one, or by the team member assigned to the work. Project team members stay busy, but important projects never get done.

Project selection is the process of identifying those projects from the array of potential projects that have the most potential for creating a positive impact on the organization. The same selection criteria can be employed to evaluate the potential costs and benefits of candidate projects or identify solution options within projects.

Because of resource constraints, no organization can implement every project that is proposed or possible. Nor should organizations adopt projects that have little potential for creating a positive outcome for the organization. As a result, organizations need to establish and apply project selection criteria that rank projects according to their net benefit and evaluate each project to determine whether that project is likely to have a positive impact. The criteria the organization employs should be transparent and understood by every person involved in the selection cycle, including project managers, project sponsors, and project evaluators.

> Some method must be applied to prioritize projects. Without explicit prioritization, priorities get set by individuals and little or nothing will get done.

Some organizations only employ financial criteria to rank projects or evaluate their merit. Financial ranking techniques include net present value and internal rate of return. Some organizations employ the payback method, which is flawed because it does not incorporate the time value of money. Payback can produce incorrect project assessments and should not be used exclusively as a project selection method.

Measuring the expected costs and benefits of a project is difficult. For that reason, many organizations employ a mixed rating system that includes financial measures and other measures, such as impact on client service or strategic impact, to weight projects. To evaluate projects, each measure is assigned a scale (e.g., one to ten) and a score assigned by evaluators. The total score for each project is calculated and compared to the other projects. That method can be tailored for each organization in order to recognize the factors that are most important.

Financial mechanisms for the selection and evaluation of projects are described in detail in Appendix 2.

These factors can be applied and rated on a cardinal scale for project evaluation:

- The relative impact on customers
- Legal requirements
- Strategic impact or strategic fit
- Financial return
- Required technology to support ongoing operations
- Ability of the technology to increase operating efficiency
- Ability to leverage technology
- Project risk
- Past results with similar projects
- Funding requirements

More sophisticated decision models can be applied dependent on the needs of the organization. The application of decision models and tools for project selection is often regarded as a separate project phase or a project in itself to be completed prior to the initiation of a project.

The following table outlines the steps of project selection using a mixed ranking system.

Step	Description
Identify decision ranking criteria	Each organization has its own set of priorities for project selection. Those responsible for project selection will need to determine why projects are undertaken, what values are important to the organization (e.g., legal compliance, flexibility, financial performance), and what criteria are most relevant to project selection. Review items on the list above and add additional criteria.
Create cardinal scales for criteria	For each criterion, an evaluation scale will need to be created. For example, if strategic impact is selected as a scoring criterion, how will that impact be converted to a numeric scale?
Assign weights to each criterion	Not all criteria are equal. It is possible to weight some more highly than others. For each criteria listed, assign a relative weight.
Assign a threshold level if needed	If appropriate, the organization can assign a threshold score below which a project will not be initiated. For example, the organization may determine that any project scoring less than twenty on its scale will not be implemented or will require further review. Exceptions for legally required projects can be made irrespective of the score.

Project Initiation

The objective of project initiation is to articulate the authorization for a project. That is typically done in a project charter document that identifies the business need and product description for the project. The project charter identifies at a very high level the need for the project, its product, and the constraints and assumptions that will guide the project. At the conclusion of the development of the project charter, a project manager is typically assigned to the project.

The project charter formally authorizes the existence of a project. It assures executive level commitment to the project, clarifies the business problem that the project will address, describes the product that needs to be created, and gives the project manager authority to allocate resources to the project. Without a project charter, the project manager cannot know for certain that adequate support has been provided for the project and cannot be certain that he or she is addressing the business need that gave rise to the project.

Project charters come in many shapes and sizes. In many cases, the charter is called by another name, including a work request. In some cases, the project charter may be verbal. If that is the case, the project manager can protect himself or herself and ensure full understanding of the intentions of management by sending a confirming letter or e-mail containing the elements of the project charter.

The project charter forms the basis of decision making about the project throughout its life.

> Each project must have some form of written authorization. If one isn't provided when the project is assigned, the project manager should write his or her own and get it approved.

Either as a part of the project charter or as a separate document, project constraints and assumptions are identified in project initiation. Project constraints are any factors that will limit the project. They include the budget and time constraints. Project assumptions are those factors that are considered to be true for project planning purposes. For example, managers may assume that a key resource will be available for the duration of the project or may assume software compatibility. Too often, project assumptions are not clearly identified, and problems are created when those unstated assumptions are no longer correct. When that happens, the ground beneath the project shifts, but no one can determine why.

It is critical that the project manager examine the project assumptions carefully and with the assistance of the project team. Those assumptions are closely related to project risks. In some cases, one person's assumptions are another person's risk factors. Assumptions should be reviewed throughout the course of the project to ensure that they are still accurate. When assumptions change, the project risk management plan may need to change as well.

In most cases, a high-level project budget and time schedule will be assigned early in the project. In an ideal world, those time and schedule constraints would be regarded as flexible until the project manager had the time to gather detailed information about the project. In practice, early budgets and time schedules are very hard to change once they are articulated.

The following table outlines the steps of project initiation.

Step	Description
Formally authorize the project	The project sponsor must formally authorize the project to start and create a project charter document. Without one, the project team does not have the authority to expend organizational resources.
Define the business need	The project charter must include the business need that the project was undertaken to address. Without a clear linkage to the business need, the project can lose its focus.
Describe the product	The project charter should include a high-level description of the product of the project (i.e., how does the organization intend to meet the business need?). The product should meet the business needs that the project was created to address.
Identify and assign a project manager	A project manager should be assigned who has the experience necessary to successfully manage and complete the project.
Identify constraints	The charter should identify and list all of the factors that will limit the project management team's options. For example, a predefined end date will limit the team's options regarding schedule and resources. The budget and schedule identified at this point in the project's life should be regarded as flexible because very little is known at this time about project details.
Identify assumptions	The charter should identify and list factors which are considered to be certain. These assumptions should be validated to assess their probability of accuracy.
Complete project charter document	To complete the document, input and feedback should be obtained from stakeholders to ensure that you did not miss any important information that may impact the success of the project.

Scope Planning

Scope planning is a process of elaborating the work of the project in greater detail than was applied to the creation of the project charter or other project enabling documents. Scope planning identifies high-level deliverables and project objectives.

The scope planning process is the first opportunity for the project manager to begin the process of developing consensus on the scope of the project. Though a project charter may be in place identifying the business need and the product of the project, the scope statement is the first declaration of the project's deliverables.

The scope statement also allows the project manager to develop a better understanding of the product of the project by applying analytic techniques to the project options. Financial analysis techniques such as those applied to project selection can be applied to assess the project alternatives.

The project manager should not develop the scope statement in a vacuum. Importantly, the preparation of the scope statement requires and inspires dialogue about the project. The result of that dialogue is consensus among the project stakeholders as to the high-level deliverables and objectives of the project.

> Most project failures are caused by poor scope definition.

High-level deliverables should be identified at the level that facilitates project planning and the development of high-level consensus about the scope of the project. Often project phases can be determined and the work of the project better organized after the high-level deliverables are identified. Objectives for the project must be measurable and will create the basis for the success or failure of the project.

The identified deliverables and objectives will form the basis for future decision making with regard to the project and for evaluating the success or failure of the project. It is possible that project changes will at some point require an adjustment of the scope statement.

The following table outlines the steps necessary for scope planning.

Step	Description
Determine if a project charter exists	If a project charter exists, it will provide the basis for development of the scope statement. The charter should contain a description of the business need and the product description.
Determine if constraints and assumptions have been identified	Constraints and assumptions are sometimes identified as part of project initiation. If they have not been, they should be created during scope planning.
Assemble a team to create a dialogue about the project scope	Like other project initiatives, scope planning should be accomplished with the input of a variety of team members and/or stakeholders. The group should not be too big so as to prevent effective operations but should be big enough to represent key viewpoints about the project. As an alternative, the project manager could write a scope statement draft and circulate it for review and comment.
Identify scope planning templates	Scope planning templates may be available in the organization or elsewhere, such as within on-line project management sites.
Refine the project justification and product description contained in the project charter. If they do not exist there, create both.	The project charter should have included a high-level description of the business need for the project and the high-level description of the product that will meet those needs. At this point, additional detail about the project may be available. That additional detail can now be reflected in the project justification and the product description.
Identify high-level project deliverables	The scope statement should include a few high-level project deliverables (five to ten). The number is dependent on the needs of the organization. Too much detail at this point will confuse the scope statement. Too little detail will limit the usefulness of the scope statement as a means of developing consensus on the project scope. Project management and the project plan can be included as deliverables. Implicitly, any items not included in project deliverables are not included within the scope of the project. If known, those exclusions should be identified and stated.

Step	Description
Identify project objectives	Project objectives are the metrics with which the overall project will be evaluated. Objectives can include time objectives, cost objectives, and quality objectives. The question that drives the establishment of objectives is this: by what criteria will we judge the success of this project?
Formalize the scope statement and circulate it for review and acceptance	The scope statement should be formalized to the extent that it can be used later as a guide to project decision making. It also forms the basis for consensus on the project scope. For that reason, it must generate the appropriate levels of approval.

Creation of the Work Breakdown Structure and Activity Definition

A Work Breakdown Structure (WBS) is used to capture project deliverables and sub-deliverables. A WBS represents graphically all project deliverables and sub-deliverables that are outcomes of a project and identifies the total scope of the project. Once the WBS is completed, activities necessary to complete the project can be identified. These activities are *verbs* that can be assigned to team members for accomplishment.

The deliverables identified in the WBS are *nouns*—things that the project must produce or create. Each successive level of the WBS represents more detail, and as a result the WBS presents a hierarchy of deliverables (nouns). It does not include activities (verbs).

> The WBS is the heart of project planning. Without it, the team has no idea what the project is intended to create.

Activity definition requires identification and documentation of the activities or tasks that must be performed to produce a successful project outcome. These activities are identified as an extension of the WBS, and the activities should culminate in the production of the deliverables and sub-deliverables that are documented in a WBS. Activities should be manageable and their attainment measurable in terms of cost and time of completion and quality of work.

The list of activities is often incorporated into project scheduling software such as Microsoft Project.

The following table outlines the steps of the development of the WBS and activity list.

Step	Description
Identify project deliverables	With the high-level deliverables in the scope statement, the project team can begin to employ decomposition to create sub-deliverables. In the course of deliverable identification, the team may decide that the scope statement requires modification.
Assign unique identifiers to all deliverable levels and deliverables	Each deliverable must be assigned a unique identifying number for tracking purposes. These numbers define the project code of accounts and allow for easy identification.
Create WBS chart	The WBS can be documented in a variety of ways but must be done in a manner that allows for a clear understanding of how the project elements fit together. The WBS becomes the most complete definition of the project scope. Any deliverables not in the WBS are not part of the scope.
Break down each deliverable into the activities (verbs) that are required to achieve it	Once a WBS identifying deliverables (nouns) is completed, those deliverables can be decomposed further by detailing the activities or tasks (verbs) that must be completed. Each activity must be understandable and able to be assigned to project staff. The extent to which activities are detailed depends on a number of factors, including the ability and experience of project team members.

Project Scheduling

In order to create a project schedule, activities must be sequenced, milestones identified, activity durations estimated, and the schedule developed by matching the activity sequence, durations, and the calendar. Schedule reports can provide a graphical representation of predicted activities, milestones, dependencies, resource requirements, activity duration, and deadlines. The project schedule should be detailed enough to show each WBS task to be performed, the name of the person responsible for completing the task, the start and end date of each task, and the expected duration of the task.

> Hard-headed realism is required for development of the project schedule. Project managers should be empowered to stand up to management pressure to commit to dates that can't be met.

The project schedule is a key part of the project plan. It needs to be committed to writing so that the project team can share and continually communicate the goals of the project. It also shows the time-related dependencies between different project tasks. In a complex project, several schedules may be necessary, covering different levels of detail or different parts of the project.

The following table outlines the steps of schedule development.

Step	Description
Sequence each activity	Using a variety of techniques, each activity is prioritized based on dependencies which may be mandatory, discretionary, or external to the activity. This is a team activity. The precedence diagramming method (PDM) is the most common technique used to create a network of all activities in the WBS, showing both dependencies and flow of activities.
Identify milestones	Milestones are key dates in every project.
Estimate the duration of each activity	This is another project team activity. Here consensus is arrived around the time required to complete each activity. Without consensus on activity duration estimates, team members may not buy in to it and may not feel responsible for meeting schedule targets. The most common technique for estimating is historical experience in projects with similar scope of work. Techniques such as top-down estimation and quantitative based estimating may also be employed.
Identify the project's critical path	This path determines the longest time it would take to complete a project given the current level of available resources. By allocating additional resources to activities in this path, the project schedule may be shortened.

Step	Description
Create the schedule	This process takes inputs from activity sequencing and prioritizing along with activity duration estimating and resource planning. There are several scheduling tools that support schedule capture like PERT and GANTT charts. For large, complex projects with a multitude of interrelated tasks, PERT charts are preferred. For smaller projects, GANTT charts are used.
Monitor project milestones and completed tasks and compare them to the plan	By comparing milestones and completed tasks with the actual project baseline schedule, one can draw a conclusion as to whether the project will be completed on schedule. Schedule status is communicated to senior management at regular intervals throughout the life of the project. It also helps determine if corrective action is required. By using earned value, it is possible to tell if the project is progressing on schedule and on budget. If a schedule variance is detected, corrective action may be necessary in order to bring the schedule into conformance with the plan by crashing or fast tracking.

Risk Planning and Tracking

Risk is inherent in every project. Effective project management requires a proactive approach to risk management with planning, identifying, assessing, and developing mitigation strategies for project risks before they impact the project. It is also important to make risk management a group activity. By including project team members, project sponsors, and project stakeholders in risk management, organizations have a better chance of identifying and resolving risks before they create adverse outcomes. In this section we review risk management and its related processes.

Project risks should be discussed at each project team meeting.

The following table outlines the steps in project risk management.

Step	Description
Develop the risk management plan and identify risks	The project plan requires a decision on how to approach and plan the risk management activities of the project and the identification of the risks of the project.
Analyze risks	This analysis is needed to identify the high ranking risks of the project. Not every risk can be responded to in a manner that balances costs and benefits.
Create a risk response plan	A risk response plan should be created for the most significant risks.
Monitor and control risks	It is important to monitor the risks of the project and identify new project risks as they need to be identified during the course of the project life cycle.

Resource Planning and Management

In order to deliver project results, the project manager must identify the resources needed for the project, acquire those resources, and manage them. Accurate resource estimates must be made for all project activities in order to establish a viable project plan and monitor project outcomes.

Resource planning also helps develop the cost and schedule estimates for the project. Program and project managers rely on these estimates to represent funding requirements to customers. Resource providers use rollups of project resource estimates to assist in determining staffing requirements and balancing the project workload.

The following table outlines the steps required for resource planning.

Step	Description
Estimate resource needs for each project activity identified at the lowest level in the WBS	Resource needs are estimated for each activity that has been created in the activity list, which is an extension of the WBS. There are several ways by which one may arrive to an estimate. Historical information on similar activities may be used or expert judgment can be sought to determine how much of each resource is need to complete the job in a given time.
Identify resources available to the project	Sometimes resources for the project will be pre-set or limited by the internal resources available. In other cases, resources from outside the organization may be available.
Identify resource availability	The availability of each resource necessary for the project must be identified.

Step	Description
Identify activities and resources that may be purchased from outside the organization	For a variety of reasons, it may suit an organization to purchase resources rather than to use its internal resources. This decision is driven by make-or-buy analysis after which management decides whether a particular product or service can be produced more cost effectively by the performing organization or by external sources.
Acquire resources	If internal resources are used, the project manager will need to negotiate with senior managers to authorize the assignment resources to each activity. This further involves organization planning, staff acquisition, and team building.

Cost Planning and Management

Project cost planning and management are employed to quantify the costs and benefits of the project and to ensure that it is completed within the budget.

Many organizations fail to make use of good cost planning and management for their projects. Often they only assign the costs of external contractors or purchases to projects and assume internal costs, which may be considerable, to be fixed. By failing to capture full project costs and by not creating cost management systems, they lose the ability to do the following:

- Compare projects
- Measure project success
- Effectively and efficiently employ resources
- Make accurate decisions about strategic initiatives
- Underestimate the effectiveness of project management initiatives

Project cost planning and management starts with cost estimating. Cost and benefit estimation begin with high level estimation techniques, like expert judgment, analogous estimating, and parametric estimating. Cost budgeting, which is the process of assigning estimated costs to activities, follows. Once those activities are assigned to a schedule, a time-phased budget is created. The time-phased budget is necessary for earned value management and cost tracking. The time-phased budget is sometimes referred to as the cost baseline.

When project work is performed, actual costs are captured and assigned to tasks. Actual cost capture is usually accomplished by the organization's accounting system. In assignment of actual, incurred costs to project activities, the organization will need to decide if it intends to capture direct costs only (those costs uniquely assignable to one project activity, such as direct labor spent on a task) or indirect costs as well. Indirect costs can include such items as facilities costs, overhead, benefits, and administrative costs. The combination of direct and indirect costs is sometimes referred to as *fully loaded* or *fully burdened* costs. The assignment of indirect costs to project activities requires the use of allocation methods.

Finally, costs need to be managed and controlled. Actual and budgeted costs are compared and actions taken to narrow variances or reduce costs. These processes are typically supported by cost accounting systems, cost allocation models, financial analysis tools, and organizational expertise in accounting, budgeting, cost allocation, and financial analysis.

The following table outlines the steps in cost management.

Step	Description
Perform high level cost and benefit estimates	At project inception or in the project selection process, high level estimates of costs and benefits are usually required. These estimates are built with very little project detail and employ methods such as analogous estimating and expert judgment to create order-of-magnitude estimates. High level cost estimation should involve several viewpoints; no one person should be accountable for making the estimate. Some variety of reality check should be applied to the estimate.
Evaluate projects, select projects from the pool of available projects, and make go/no-go decisions	Project evaluation is part of the project selection process.
Identify the resources necessary for the project	Based on the WBS and the activity definitions that flow from it, resource requirements for the project are identified and acquired. This should be a team activity. In some cases, resources will be pre-assigned to the project. In other cases, the project manager may have the ability to assemble a project team. Make-or-buy decisions may be involved in resource planning. The objective is to identify the most cost-effective method of procuring the appropriate resources. Other factors that might cause an organization to use in-house resources over external resources are the need for control over the project and the extent to which the information necessary for the project is proprietary.

Step	Description
Perform detailed cost estimation	Based on the detailed resource requirements and the WBS, the costs of the resources necessary to complete the project are identified. Techniques such as bottom-up estimating and activity-based costing are employed for detailed estimates. Detailed cost estimation is a team activity that requires several viewpoints and the development of consensus. Without consensus on cost estimates, team members may not buy in to the estimates and may not feel responsible for meeting cost targets.
Assign estimated costs to activities and time periods to create the time-phased budget	If activity-based costing has been employed for detailed cost estimating, costs will have been automatically assigned to activities. If costs have been estimated using some other technique, they will have to be allocated to the activities of the project to create the cost baseline and to allow earned value calculations.
Collect actual direct project costs and assign indirect costs to the project	If direct costs, such as labor costs, aren't captured by the accounting system, an off-line system will have to be created to gather direct project costs. That can be accomplished with simple spreadsheet applications. Some organizations only collect direct costs for projects. Others also assign indirect costs to projects. Indirect costs may include facilities costs and administrative costs. If the organization intends to allocate indirect costs to projects, it will need to identify the indirect costs to allocate, establish allocation bases (such as percentage of square footage used by the project or direct costs incurred), and allocate the captured indirect costs using the allocation bases.
Compare actual to budgeted costs and take corrective action if needed	Actual project costs will need to be compared to budgeted project costs to determine if corrective action is needed. The best method for comparison of actual to budgeted costs is earned value because of its ability to segregate schedule variances from cost variances. Without earned value, it is impossible to tell if cost savings are related to efficiency or if the project is behind schedule. If a cost variance is detected, corrective action may be necessary in order to bring costs into conformance with the plan. Alternatively, budgets may be revised to reflect more accurate assessments. With actual cost data in hand, it may be useful to attempt to predict the estimated costs it will take to complete the project. Again, earned value allows the best estimation of the cost of project completion.

Effective Project Communications

Communications planning is employed in order to identify project stakeholders and develop a plan to meet their communications needs throughout the project's lifespan. The communications plan is essential to building and maintaining project buy-in by key stakeholders. Communications planning also is closely related to scope planning and definition as those processes are essential to ensuring that stakeholders fully understand the deliverables the project will create.

Effective communications often make the difference between project success and project failure. Without effective communications, project stakeholders can lose interest in the project, develop unreasonable expectations or unreasonable fears, fall out of the loop, and become surprised by project results or progress.

Much of the project planning process is focused on project communications. Standard project documents, like the scope statement, the charter, and the WBS are designed to create an effective project dialogue and to communicate details of the project to the appropriate stakeholders. As a result, it is difficult to distinguish where project communications and other project activities diverge.

Estimates suggest that the majority of the work of a project manager is communication. Those who communicate well, using varied means, often manage their projects successfully. Those project managers who regard their principal function to be the management of the team and creation of project documents will often come up short because external project stakeholders have not been adequately communicated with and because their needs haven't been identified and addressed.

Project stakeholders include anyone affected by the project, involved in it, or who has the ability to influence it. That definition casts a wide net which includes the project team, senior managers, the sponsor, users of the product of the project, other external stakeholders who might be impacted, regulatory agencies that can influence the project, and a host of others. Identifying stakeholder needs is a key though challenging process. Often stakeholders will not be able to clearly articulate their needs or their interests. In those cases the project manager must engage the stakeholders in a facilitated process to elicit those needs and interests.

One valuable tool for the identification of stakeholder needs is distinguishing between stakeholder positions and interests. Positions are often clearly stated by the stakeholder as a "must have" statement. Stakeholder positions often conflict with one another. A better way to address stakeholder needs is to attempt to identify the interests behind the stated needs.

Another way to identify stakeholder interests is to examine the potential emotional reactions that the project may engender. All too often, project managers make the assumption that they can convince project stakeholders that their lives will become better or easier through the application of the product of their projects. They presume that stakeholders will respond intellectually to the project and see its value. They assume that communication of the business logic of the project and project status is all that is necessary to ensure buy-in to what they see as a meritorious effort and a useful product.

What project managers fail to take into account is that people respond both intellectually and emotionally to projects that will impact their lives. While intellectual responses are predictable and amenable to reason, emotional responses are much harder to predict and can lead to stakeholder reactions that may seem to be unreasonable and unwarranted.

At the heart of these emotional responses are the project *fear factors*, those stakeholder responses driven by fear rather than intellect. Those fear factors can take a simple automation project and convert it to a threat on the livelihood or professional standing of the user. Other fear factors might include the fear of greater levels of accountability, the fear of job loss, the fear of being unable to cope with the technology which might also lead to a threat to employment, a fear that the technology will make work harder and therefore more demanding than it is currently, and a fear that the technology will change the nature of the work and damage the self-image of the user.

> Project managers need to keep in mind that stakeholders respond intellectually and emotionally to projects. Those emotional responses cannot be ignored.

If project managers fail to recognize these fear factors, they may be blindsided by stakeholder reactions. Fortunately, with work these fear factors can be identified, and once identified, can be addressed.

Successful project communications must address both intellectual and emotional reactions to their projects. Successful project managers can use the fear factors to create project communications that create comfort with the project and build buy-in by heading off resistance caused by the emotional responses.

Once the project team has identified the stakeholders and their interests, they can identify methods for meeting the communications needs of those stakeholders. A variety of methods are available for communicating with stakeholders. They can employ standard project reports (Gantt charts, milestone charts, project network diagrams, the WBS) and other means, which might include newsletters, presentations, individualized correspondences, and face-to-face briefings.

Through the course of the project, the needs and interests of the stakeholders may change. That fact is compounded by the fact that the project itself may evolve over time as requirements and business needs change. That will create an evolution of project buy-in as stakeholders who were onboard reassess their opinions and interests. In other cases, the stakeholders themselves may change in the midst of the project. The project manager should not make the presumption that new stakeholders will have the same interests and level of commitment to the project that their successors had.

Once the communications plan is created, it becomes a part of the overall project plan, subject to change as necessary. The communications plan also drives information dissemination, the process of actually distributing necessary project information.

The project manager also needs to be aware of aspects of the organization's culture with regard to reporting and information dissemination. Some organizations rely more heavily on presentations, some on written reports, and others on visual representations, like charts and graphs. Some organizations require lengthy reports; others place a premium on brevity.

Last, project communications requires the effective closure of the project. At the close of the project, lessons learned should be documented and project records collected and appropriately filed. At project closeout, contracts should be closed and project team members reassigned.

The following table outlines the steps in project communications.

Step	Description
Identify project stakeholders	Project stakeholders include those impacted by the results or performance of the project, those who are actively involved in its planning or execution, and those who can influence the project, either positively or negatively. The project team may participate in stakeholder identification. Stakeholders can be internal to the organization or external to it.
Identify stakeholder interests	Once a stakeholder list is compiled, each stakeholder should be analyzed to determine their interests in the project. In addition, a fear factor analysis should be conducted to determine the types of emotional reactions stakeholders may have with regard to the project. Any assumed stakeholder interests should be validated by conversation with the stakeholder.

Step	Description
Create a communications plan	Based on the stated and implied needs and interests of the stakeholders, a communications plan should be created. That plan should identify how information will be disseminated to stakeholders and by what means and frequency, how information will be accessed and filed, and any other information relevant to project communications. The length and level of detail of the plan should be based on the needs of the organization. All information dissemination must pass a cost-benefit test (i.e., is the value of the communication worth its cost?).
Disseminate information according to the plan and respond to unexpected requests for information	Information dissemination requires implementation of the communications plan. Information dissemination may be by verbal presentation, written reports, formal communications, or informal communications. The needs of stakeholders are the key determinants of how information is distributed.
Measure project performance against the project plan	If the project plan is appropriately constructed, the progress of the project can be measured against it. That requires clear quality metrics and adequate data to measure time and cost performance. As noted earlier, earned value is the best measure of project performance. If variances between the project's performance and project plan are identified, corrective action must be taken. That corrective action can include the modification of the plan to reflect performance to date.
Close the project	Project closeout is the process of bringing the project to an orderly close. In project closeout, all contracts should be closed, project results documented, project records assembled and stored, lessons learned identified and documented, and staff reassigned.

Performance Reporting

Project performance measurements are employed to ensure that the project meets its goals on schedule, within budget and with the best possible quality. To accomplish that goal, performance measurement consists of the following:

- Establishing appropriate and measurable project objectives
- Identifying and articulating product requirements and specifications
- Comparing project and product outcomes to the project plan and product requirements to identify variances
- Analyzing performance using appropriate tools and techniques
- Performance reporting
- Taking corrective action

Unfortunately, many organizations fail to adequately measure project performance against objective criteria. One key to effective performance management is fostering an organizational culture that values and rewards performance and accountability.

Performance measurement first requires that clear and measurable objectives be created for the project and the product of the project. This is typically accomplished during project scope planning. Objectives must be capable of being measured; they must be quantifiable. They must also be clear so that everyone understands the objective and they must be relevant to the project or its product. Objectives can include time, cost, and quality objectives. If possible, subjective criteria should be avoided. Identifying objectives for project phases also allows for earlier warning of potential problems. Assigning costs and activity durations to each activity provides the best means of tracking cost and time objectives.

The requirements for the product of the project are defined during project requirements gathering. These requirements must also be clear and measurable, which is often a challenge. If measurable objectives have been identified, project performance can be measured against those objectives to identify variances. Those variances can be analyzed using a variety of tools and techniques. They include earned value management, a powerful tool for performance management that links schedule and cost performance. Other performance management techniques include trend analysis and performance reviews.

> That which is measured gets managed. Without metrics, we have no way of identifying project success or failure or of learning from our experiences.

Following analysis, the performance of the project can be reported to stakeholders. Performance reporting may include written reports, formal presentations, and informal reports. The objective of performance measurement and reporting is not to blame individuals for poor performance. The objective is to find opportunities for performance improvement and to take corrective action.

Last, performance management allows for the identification of lessons learned for the project that can be passed on to other project managers in order to increase the project management capability of the organization.

The following table outlines the steps of project performance measurement.

Step	Description
Creating a detailed project scope statement	The scope statement provides detail on the business need for the project. The principal performance metric for the project is its ability to meet the needs of business users.
Identify project objectives	Project objectives are quantitative metrics of project performance. Cost and time objectives are fairly simple to identify. Quality or scope objectives are more complex. Examples may include meeting federal environmental standards or meeting user requirements as measured by user satisfaction indices.
Identify product requirements	Requirement identification is described in another section of this chapter.
Identify variances between the project plan and project outcomes	A detailed project plan allows comparison between actual results and the plan. Put another way, project variances are differences between the desired state and the actual state of project performance.
Analyze variances	Several techniques are available to analyze variances. The most effective is earned value analysis. Earned value analysis requires that each activity be assigned an estimated cost and that each activity be scheduled. Other techniques for analyzing variances include performance reviews and trend analysis. Performance reviews can be scheduled at regular intervals or may be conducted as needed. Trend analysis attempts to identify the impact of variances on the remainder of the project. Extensions of earned value analysis allow the impact of variances experienced to date to be forecasted.

Step	Description
Report performance to appropriate stakeholders	Having identified those stakeholders who need to be informed of project variances, performance can be reported using presentations, standard reports, and one-time reports. The project communications plan describes the plan for reporting to stakeholders.
Take corrective action to close variances	The goal of performance measurement is to identify the corrective action that is needed to bring project performance back into conformance with the project plan. A variety of corrective actions may be available and may include fast tracking or crashing the schedule, searching for ways to reduce project expenditures, and modifying the project scope.
Identify lessons learned	Lessons learned allow the organization to learn from its successes and failures.

Project Change Control

Project change management is the process of determining which requested changes to the product will be made, when they will be made, and the impact they will have on the project deliverables and the project. It is used to limit and coordinate requirements and specification changes that arise during the life of a project. The objective of this process is to prevent all but necessary project changes.

A common cause of project overruns is uncontrolled changes in product specifications, leading to the expansion of the project scope. These are the underlying concepts of change management:

- Since changes are inevitable, they must be managed very carefully to ensure the project is completed in a timely manner.

- Changes and change control require effort, which must be estimated and factored into the plan.

- Any requirement changes and specification changes that arise after specifications have been frozen should be postponed unless they are high priority (i.e., the system will not function without the changes) or postponement will cause significant avoidable costs later.

- The change management process, including prioritization criteria and the change control committee members, should be agreed upon early in the project.

The following table outlines the steps of project change control.

Step	Description
Document change requests	Any changes that are requested to requirements or designs that have been reviewed, approved, and placed under change control require documentation.
Assess change requests	All change requests must be assessed for impact.
Review change requests with the team	Assessment of the change request should be accomplished prior to team review.
Document change impacts	Appropriate documentation of the impact of change will be included in the associated change management log.
Review change requests by project sponsors	Once assessment is complete, the request will be reviewed by project sponsors.
Approve or reject change requests	Change requests can be approved or rejected.
Document approval	Approval should be documented for tracking purposes.
Implement changes if approved	Approved changes can be assigned to appropriate project personnel and implemented. Changes in the project plan have to be made to reflect the change.

Project Closure

Project closure is employed at the end of the project and also at the end of each phase in the project life cycle. It is intended to bring the project or the phase to an orderly close, whether due to completion or termination. It includes the processes of acceptance and turn over of project deliverables to operations, resource redistribution, financial accounts close out, archival of project records, documentation of lessons learned, and post-implementation review.

The project team needs to fight the urge to skip project closure.

All too often, projects are not ended in an organized or orderly manner. Often by the time project closure is considered, the resources of the project have been expended; project personnel are interested in moving on to another project, project deliverables have been produced, and the project manager has been reassigned. As a result, appropriate project documentation is not created and filed and the lessons learned from the project are not documented for the benefit of future projects.

The major focus of project closure is the assembly of project documentation and archiving that information in a form that allows retrieval. In order for a project to be properly closed, the lessons learned from that project must be passed on to other project managers for their use in similar projects. Only with codified lessons learned can an organization learn from its experiences and increase its project management maturity level.

The following table outlines the steps of project closure.

Step	Description
Review deliverable documentation	Deliverable specifications are obtained as part of the project requirements specification process.
Review project status and performance documentation	Both the performance and status of the project are obtained during the executing and controlling process of the project life cycle.
Turn over deliverables to operations	Acceptance is based on terms as defined in the scope and requirements of the project. Once the project objectives have been met, a formal or informal sign-off on the project deliverable may be required.
Celebrate successes	This is a team activity. Team and individual performances are recognized and rewarded based on organizational policies.
Redistributing resources	All resources assigned to the project are temporary and must be released from the project.
Close out financial accounts	All outstanding accounts with regards to project activities are balanced and closed out. Audits may be carried out per organizational practices

Step	Description
Review the project for lessons learned	This post-implementation review looks at the project output irrespective of its success or failure. Depending on the size and investment in the project, this may be a large group activity involving senior management, the project team, and support staff. For smaller projects this would just include the project team and support staff. All valid feedback, problems identified and their solutions are documented for future reference. Wherever possible, lessons learned must be translated into procedures that can be used in future projects.
Completing, collecting, and archiving project records	All documentation with regard to the project is archived. This historical data serves to help improve future projects.

Summary and Conclusions

For an organization to make use of effective project management, it needs to create standardized processes, and those processes need to be tailored to address the unique needs of the organization. They should also be scalable to the largest and smallest projects of the organization.

A set of project management standards has been developed by PMI and documented in its *PMBOK® Guide*. Whether that method is tailored to the needs of the organization or another method is used, the method must be communicated throughout the organization and its use mandated.

> **Jump-Starting the Project Initiative**
> **Standard Processes**
>
> - Identify existing processes.
> - Determine how projects are selected and prioritized.
> - Create a process for identifying project scope.
> - Evaluate established processes such as those identified by PMI for application to your environment.
> - Develop templates for key processes.
> - Provide training in the chosen methodology.

Case Study: A Financial Services Company
Building Standard Project Management Processes

A financial services company saw the need to improve its project management processes, particularly in its information technology operations. It established a PMO, located within the IT department, which attempted to employ an enterprise project management system. That system failed to be used as intended. Ultimately, the PMO was eliminated.

Several years later, the company reinstituted its PMO. This time, however, the PMO was situated at the corporate level. The project manager assigned to manage the PMO had been successful in a number of company projects and was familiar with the company's operations and management structure. He was also a PMP®.

Instead of focusing on the use of an EPM tool, the PMO recruited several well-respected project managers and started taking on the company's toughest projects. In some cases, operating divisions requested that the PMO take over their most critical projects. While the PMO gathered credibility, the manager of the PMO assumed the role of "selling" project management to senior managers throughout the company.

As his next step in building the company's project management capacity, the PMO manager built a set of project management processes and templates. Those processes and templates were tailored to fit the company's needs.

Today, the PMO manager continues to build support for project management throughout the company. Now, with strong senior-level support, project successes under his belt, and customized project management processes in place, the PMO director is beginning to evaluate EPM systems.

CHAPTER 7

The Application of Project Management Tools

In the project management profession, it is understood that there is no such thing as project management software. By that they mean that no software can manage a project. Only project managers can manage projects.

Nonetheless, there are software tools that can aid the project manager. At low levels of project management maturity, project management software is not generally used, or if it is used, each project manager chooses his or her own favorite tool. As the project management maturity of the organization increases, standardization of the tool is critical for sustaining the long term viability of the initiative and for measuring the impacts of project management as a management tool. In most cases, standardizing a tool across the organization will reduce software costs and improve the ability of the organization to manage and monitor its projects.

In this chapter, we will consider two issues related to the choice of a software tool for project management:

- The features and limitations of most project management software
- The application of enterprise-wide project management software

Project Management Software

All too often, organizations inexperienced in project management conclude that all that they need to improve their ability to deliver projects on time, on budget, and with the desired functionality is to purchase and employ project management software. Though they may improve their ability to create Gantt charts and find the critical path, they usually don't see dramatic improvements in project performance.

> Too often organizations presume that a project management tool will solve all of the organization's project problems.

Project management software can be very useful, especially for project managers managing complex projects with substantial numbers of tasks. Project management software is also useful for those projects with complex dependencies that may not be fully obvious without analysis.

Project management software can help the project manager track milestone dates and tasks. Most software also helps the project manager identify and track task dependencies and the critical path as well as resources (human and materials) assigned to complete the tasks. It can also provide easy, formatted reports showing tasks on schedule or behind schedule and resources that are overloaded. Complex analysis, such as earned value analysis and variance analysis, can also be automated within these packages, allowing the project manager to focus on the "soft side" of project management without spending all of his or her time managing the project schedule, budget, and reporting.

Project management software is not the answer to every project management problem. Project managers who manage their projects in the software can become detached from the real world and fail to establish the relationships necessary for getting the work done. Those that rely on the status reports created by the software as their predominant or only means of communicating about the project may discover that they have created dissatisfied stakeholders and lost the support they need. Even if detailed project plans and status reports are prepared using the tool, it doesn't mean that they'll be read by managers. Project managers that get tied up too deeply in the details run the risk of losing sight of the big picture.

Project management software may also confuse the differences between deliverables and activities. As you will recall, deliverables are nouns and the things that the project creates. They are identified at a high level by the scope statement and defined at a detailed level within the creation of the work breakdown structure, arguably the most important step in the project planning process. Activities are verbs and are only defined after the work breakdown structure has been created. Activities can be broken down further into tasks.

> There is a lot of project planning that needs to be done before the software is installed or opened.

Unfortunately, most project management software begins with the identification of tasks, getting the proverbial cart before the horse. Though experienced project managers know to delay the identification of tasks until well into the planning process, less experienced managers may be tempted to make the mistake of trying to define tasks before they have thoroughly defined the project's scope.

Standardization of a project management tool across the organization is a step toward increasing the project management maturity of the organization and can have the advantages of reducing overall software costs, simplifying software support, standardizing project planning templates, and providing a common framework within which project status is understood. It also allows for a more targeted and focused training program for new project managers.

The choice of a standard project management tool can, however, alienate some managers who are used to other tools. If a tool is chosen, support for the use of the tool, training, and incentives for its use must be provided by managers for those who are expected to apply it.

Enterprise-Wide Project Management Software

Enterprise Project Management (EPM) software is a powerful, feature-rich tool for planning, coordinating, and tracking projects. An EPM is not appropriate for every organization and can be a challenge for some organizations to install and employ.

The challenges that organizations face as they attempt to employ an EPM are technical, human, and organizational. The most difficult are the organizational challenges. This section discusses challenges to successful use of an EPM by identifying the ideal organizational candidate for it and what can be done if your organization strays from that ideal.

> Though an EPM can be a very useful tool, make sure that your organization is ready for one before you make the investment.

An EPM can help organizations make better use of their assets and manage their projects more successfully. However, they are not for the faint-of-heart and pose substantial implications for the way that organizations are structured and managed. They can be a catalyst for sweeping organizational change if implemented as part of a larger, more comprehensive initiative to change the way the organization operates. For the organization that is not ready for an

EPM and that doesn't recognize the considerable operational changes that may be required, it may present an insurmountable challenge.

An EPM cannot substitute for solid organizational processes and systems, nor can it replace good relationships and effective communications, but an EPM, the pinnacle of project management software, has the capability to address significant organizational project management pain points. It has the potential to create more uniform project management, control resource management, and enable portfolio management. It can facilitate collaboration and communications to unite managers, executives, team members, customers, and partners. It can improve the ability to tailor project reports and views.

Most importantly, an EPM can help to align projects with corporate strategy. Project tracking and resource optimization are centrally housed, which helps to streamline project management processes across an organization. A centralized EPM can also increase collaboration and knowledge-sharing across the organization, in part to offset geographical separation. These are laudable goals that many organizations aspire to achieve. For larger organizations in fast-moving, competitive markets, they are imperatives.

> Many organizations employ an EPM for better management of resources. Though they can help with coordination of resources, they can't improve project management skills or make up for a shortage of good resources.

Nonetheless, not all organizations are well-suited for the installation of an EPM. An EPM is not simply a tool for rolling up project data to a central location. It is a tool for enabling a fundamental change in the way that most organizations operate. The organization that is ideal for implementation must have several key capabilities and be relatively mature in its application of project management. The organization that is best-suited for effective application of an EPM should score well on each of the attributes listed below.

Top-to-Bottom Support for the EPM Initiative

It's not enough for senior managers to force an EPM onto the organization, though their support is required. Without support for the initiative at the project manager level, the EPM implementation might be impeded by overt and covert opposition or sabotage. The implementation of an EPM should enhance the ability of project managers to manage their projects; it should not require activities that they view as unproductive. Project team members also need to make the use of an EPM part of their daily routine; schedules must be kept current and time must be entered into time tracking systems.

In the real world, initiatives are sometimes imposed from the top of the organization in an attempt to force the organization into being what it is not. Despite the best intentions of senior managers, a disconnection can develop between them and those who make the organization operate on a daily basis and at the customer interface. Senior managers need to identify the informal networks in their organizations—networks that are sometimes referred to as "communities of practice." Those communities exercise considerable power and will be discussed in more detail in Chapter 9. In addition, leadership operates at all levels of an organization, not just from the top. The support of leaders throughout the organization is critical to the success of any initiative, including the initiative to implement an EPM.

Highly Developed Human Resource Capacity

The maintenance of a resource pool requires sophisticated human resource systems. Identifying measurable skill sets and legitimate gradations among them is a challenging task. Those identified skill sets and the system for assigning gradations must be legally defensible and able to be applied without adding crippling administrative costs. Performance rating systems and testing systems are necessary for confirming the existence of the skills and for upgrading the resource pool to keep it current.

The use of a resource pool implies that the skill sets of the named resources can be identified and quantified. Some skill sets are also far easier to quantify. For example, it is easier to identify the skill sets of technology staff than it is to identify and evaluate the skill sets of human resource professionals. That skill inventory must also be updated frequently to be kept current. Homogenous skill sets, which also imply a relatively homogenous product line, also make the cataloging easier; an organization with very diverse product lines will experience greater cataloguing challenges because of the wider array of skills in the organization and may experience greater resistance to sharing resources. For example, a law firm may have an easier time developing a resource pool than a consulting firm with a broad array of service offerings. In addition, most organizations do not spend enough time creating and maintaining strong human resource systems. If staff evaluation systems are in place, they are often ignored, out of date, or "gamed" by managers who want to support their staff by providing good evaluations for mediocre performance. Few organizations can quantify skill sets and measure the performance of their staff persons against those skill sets. That is particularly the case for organizations that employ highly diverse skill sets and large numbers of persons whose value is determined by their application of soft skills, like communicating effectively and managing conflict, which are the most critical skills for project success.

Solid Accounting Systems

Accounting systems must accumulate project costs, including the costs of internal staff, and allocate those costs to projects. The project cost-tracking feature of EPM systems and good project cost data can provide powerful information for measuring project progress and success. Many organizations don't do a good job of managing costs. Cost estimates might be prepared as a part of the project plan or project selection, but actual costs are sometimes not tracked once the project is selected.

Many organizations have poorly developed project accounting systems. Most damaging is the common practice of assuming that internal staff resources are free to projects. Too often, only the costs of external resources are assigned to projects. The true cost of projects is obscured and it is impossible to prioritize projects based on their real return on investment. Though an estimate of costs and benefits may be made prior to a project's initiation, accumulation and analysis of actual costs incurred in the project is less common.

A Solid Management Structure

The management structure of the organization needs to allow sharing across the organization and mitigate *siloing* or *empire building*. The benefits of an EPM are greatest if the portfolio of projects and resource sharing extend across the entire organization or at least the entire business unit. Driving use of the system requires buy-in by unit managers who understand the value of a shared resource pool and a centrally managed resource allocation process.

Many organizations have relatively autonomous divisions or units that operate independently and management structures and reward systems that discourage resource sharing. If managers see an advantage in hoarding valuable resources, they will resist making them available to projects that benefit other units. Resistance to the use of an EPM may be overt or covert, but in either case, managers must be provided incentives to make an EPM work. In those autonomous units, project management processes and maturity may also differ. Creating uniform project management systems is critical to the effective application of an EPM across the enterprise.

Clearly Identified Projects

In order to employ an EPM most effectively, an organization has to be able to clearly identify its projects and, in the best circumstances, drive the assignment of work through projects. No project management software can be effective if the organization can't recognize and define its projects. In many organizations, projects are not well-defined. Without processes for initiating or closing projects, the number of open projects grows. Many of those projects have no clear scope, success criteria, manager, and resources assigned. An organization cannot employ an enterprise project management system if there is no way to identify the organization's projects. Even if an EPM is implemented, some managers may want to keep their pet projects below the radar.

A Relatively High Level of Project Management Maturity

An EPM will function best in organizations at relatively high levels of project management maturity. Some would argue that organizations at Levels One and Two of project management maturity models, where in fact most organizations reside, cannot make productive use of an enterprise project management system. An EPM requires a commitment to project management; higher levels of project management maturity serve to indicate that that commitment is in place in the organization. See Appendix 1 for a tool for quickly assessing your organization's project management maturity level.

Most organizations operate at low levels of project management maturity. They may not have standard project management processes, trained and experienced project managers, project selection methods, or even a clear definition of what a project is. An EPM will not by itself improve the project management maturity of the organization.

> Those who don't feel that their organizations are ready for an EPM shouldn't lose heart. Getting ready for the application of an EPM can be a good driver for driving organizational change.

Most, if not all, organizations would like to embody the positive characteristics listed above and would like to believe that they are ideal for an EPM installation, but most fall short. Installing an EPM will not make them what they are not, though, as we will discuss later, installing an EPM can provide an opportunity for inducing organizational change.

An attempt to install and use an EPM can also have the effect of exposing an organization's weaknesses and shortcomings. Without an understanding of the organizational requirements and implications, it can be a frustrating and humbling experience.

So what is an organization to do? Should they forget about employing an EPM?

Organizations which are not ready for a full-scale implementation of an EPM have several choices which are described below.

Standardize Only Desktop Versions of Project Management Software

For some organizations, an EPM may not be an effective solution. Those organizations may not manage projects well, may not have a commitment to project management or the use of an EPM, and may not be prepared for the investment that is required.

For them, and for organizations at lower levels of project maturity, desktop versions of project management software can be very effectively employed.

Postpone the Application of the EPM until the Organization's Maturity Increases

It is possible that a relatively immature organization may increase its capabilities over time to the point where an EPM makes more sense. Those improvements require a commitment to improving their project management maturity, which requires time and resources. Without that commitment improvement is only wishful thinking. If the implementation of an EPM is a future goal, the organization can begin planning now for developing the capacity required.

Implement an EPM with Limited Functionality

If the organization can identify its most critical needs, it can implement those features and functions in an EPM first, postponing the full implementation of it. Unfortunately, resource management is a function high on the wish list of many organizations. The resource management function within an EPM requires the pre-existence of several key systems described above and may not be the easiest stand-alone function to install.

Implement the System in Only a Portion of the Organization

Project management processes may not be standardized across the organization, and the organization may not be prepared for enterprise-wide integration. However, there may still be sub-units of the organization where an EPM can be productively employed.

Employ an EPM as Part of a Comprehensive Program of Organizational Change

With a clear-eyed assessment of the capabilities of the organization and the requirements for effective application of an EPM, an organization can employ the implementation of an EPM as a catalyst for organizational change. An EPM will not make the organization change, but if a change initiative is implemented along with the software installation, the two efforts can create synergistic results and amplify the effect of the change.

> Implementing the technology required for an EPM is the easy part. The organizational and human challenges are much tougher.

That comprehensive program of change will require the technical skills necessary to install and optimize an EPM and the soft skills necessary to create effective processes and methods to support the software. It will also require a cultural shift in the organization to embrace project management as a way of organizational life.

Summary and Conclusions

In combination, project management maturity, solid management systems, and project management software can produce solid results.

For some organizations the application of an EPM is the natural, next step in their project management evolution. It presents for them the ability to integrate the good project systems and processes that they have built and the chance to manage their projects as a comprehensive portfolio.

For other organizations, an EPM will present a larger challenge. At the same time, however, it presents them an opportunity and a focal point for their efforts to improve their project management maturity.

Irrespective of the option for installation adopted by the organization, that effort, like every other project, requires a project plan and good project management. That plan, driven by a careful identification and documentation of the project's requirements, also needs to have an achievable scope and careful risk analysis prior to loading the first software program.

Jump-Starting the Project Initiative Project Management Software
• Identify existing project management software availability and use. • Identify a tool to standardize. • Provide training on the use of the tool. • Assess the organization's need for and capacity to install and employ an EPM. • Identify an implementation strategy (from those listed in this chapter).

CHAPTER 8

Organizational Structures for Successful Project Management

Even with the best training, processes, and tools, project management initiatives are likely to founder if the organization isn't structured to support project managers. All too often project managers can become frustrated by organizational inertia and organizational politics and ultimately give up.

Sometimes project managers even get the impression that the organization has arrayed itself against them. Though lip service is paid to managing projects well and providing project managers with the authority they need, it sometimes appears to project managers that they have to fight the organization and functional managers, who are trying to protect their turf at every turn. Sometimes even the PMO that has been created to remove organizational barriers can be perceived as a barrier itself.

In some cases, even providing training to project managers can frustrate them if they conclude that the organization won't support the application of their new knowledge. They may go through the motions and attend mandatory project management training, but the energy they expend on the application of project management tools and methods will be constrained by a "why bother" attitude.

In this chapter, we will consider the ways that an organization can structure itself to better support project management by examining:

- The importance of aligning the organization with the goals of effective project management
- The assignment of responsibility to the project manager, which can be a threat to functional managers
- The interaction between processes and projects in an organization
- Three common organizational mechanisms for managing projects better:
  o Functional versus "projectized" organizations

o Project management offices

o Committees and review boards to manage project selection and changes

No organization is perfect, and project managers will always have to cope with the reality of organizational politics. But organizations can take steps to reduce the impediments to successful project management. Unfortunately, most organizations embarking on an initiative to improve the way they manage projects fail to address organizational issues and fail to achieve the results they seek.

Organizational Alignment for Project Management

In today's fast-paced and rapidly changing economy, organizations are attempting to find better mechanisms for delivering results with limited resources. They are finding that the traditional, pyramidal organization model is too rigid, too slow, and too often disconnected from customers. That is particularly the case when the organization is dependent for its survival on the successful delivery of strategic projects.

That does not mean that those traditional organizations have disappeared. In a lot of organizations, managers are fighting rearguard actions to retain their power even though the pressures for change are significant. They will eventually lose those battles. In a fast-paced, results-oriented organization, positions, titles, and the corner office someday will not be indicators of status.

Eventually, status will be determined by the ability to get things done. That is why many organizations are employing project management to improve their chances of defeating entrenched bureaucracies and spanning organizational silos.

Despite the best intentions of a project management initiative, that initiative will not achieve its intended results unless the organization recognizes the importance of project management and builds mechanisms for project management into its structure. The structure of an organization can impede effective project management by creating impediments to the assignment of competent staff to projects. It can make cross-functional and cross-organizational communications difficult and limit the real authority of project managers.

Project managers are responsible for project performance as a whole but sometimes do not own their project staff and are unable to reward or punish individual performance on the project team. This structure essentially makes the project manager's job that of attempting to control the uncontrollable, which often leads to both project failure and project manager frustration.

Support of project management has to be built into the incentive systems for both managers and staff. Managers must understand the importance of allowing staff to work on projects and the need to share their authority with the project management structure. They have to learn to not fear project managers and to not see them as a threat to their turf or authority.

> One of the biggest threats to project accomplishment is the "real job" that project team members have. That job often still demands their attention and time and gets in the way of their project work.

Similarly, the staff members of the organization need to understand the importance of projects and project management. In many organizations, project team members hold allegiance to their "real" jobs in comparison to their project assignments. Their reward systems are usually connected to their permanent jobs rather than their project assignments, unless, of course, project assignments are full-time and permanent.

Creating an environment that is conducive to project management requires that the organization make a serious commitment to it. That kind of commitment is not likely to occur unless the goals of project management can be tied to the strategic direction of the organization. Like an armada, all of the organization's elements have to be made to sail in the same direction, a difficult undertaking in the world of business or government or at sea.

An organization can begin to create the necessary commitment to project management by sending a clear message to project managers that they are highly valued and that project management is a legitimate career path. Successful project performance should be tied to an incentive plan that will drive positive project behaviors from project managers and project team members. Additionally, the organization should communicate the value of project management and project managers to existing functional or line managers.

There will always be those who do not see the wisdom of an emphasis on project management. With clear acknowledgement of the importance of projects to the organization, however, adversity and resistance can be minimized to the point where those opposed are outliers in the organization and do not threaten the success of projects.

Assignment of Project Management Responsibility and Accountability

Ultimately, project management is about designating someone as being responsible for project outcomes. Unfortunately, a major issue in many organizations is the assignment of responsibility for project management. In an ideal world in which senior managers are strongly committed to project management and project success, the project manager would be given complete responsibility and authority to deliver project results.

Two problems may occur when project management responsibility is initially assigned. First, existing functional managers may be fearful of giving up responsibility. They might like the idea of project management in concept, but the reality of having someone with enough authority to compel results across organizational boundaries can be a threat. Rarely will they admit to fearing the assignment of authority to project managers, but their adversity will be a factor nonetheless in limiting the ability of project managers to get things done.

The second problem, which is related to the first, is disagreement about the definition of what a project manager is and does. Often, we hear managers say, "Let's assign Bob as the project manager. It won't take much of his time; all he has to do is develop a schedule and do periodic status reports."

> Project management can be frightening to functional managers and can pose a threat to their authority.

Those managers confuse project management with project coordination or project administration, which are lesser assignments than project management. Too often, project managers lament that they were given the title but never had the authority necessary to marshal the resources necessary for the project, control those resources, or get the job done.

In most organizations, project managers will never get the full range of authority they desire. In an ideal organization, project managers would have the ability to choose the resources, including team members, they believe they need. They should also be able to assign tasks and priorities to team members as well as reward and punish team performance as appropriate. Project managers need to have access to senior managers and ensure that they will make decisions about project direction, priorities, and scope in a timely manner. This type of authority would allow the project manager to manage the project within the approved project plan, manage the performance of vendors, and establish quality standards across the project and project team.

Though most organizations will limit project manager authority to some degree (no one wants to create "project dictators"), organizations should make project manager authority explicit and provide clear indication that project performance is a high priority.

A full system of project accountability includes identifying the relationship of the project manager to the project's stakeholders, assigning project roles, and documenting responsibilities for the project. Most organizations undertake more than one project at a time, which can create confusion regarding roles and responsibilities. One person might be the manager of several projects and simultaneously be a team member on several others. If you couple that complexity with unclear project definitions and staff turnover, you can create near-chaos and a situation where no one is ultimately responsible for projects or project tasks.

> Though it sounds obvious, the authority of the project manager must be explicit. The organization should not assume that everyone has the same definition of project management.

Assigning and documenting project accountability provides a foundation on which the project structure is built. It sets up guidelines regarding who has what level of authority to make decisions, who will be involved in the project, who will be impacted by the project, and who can influence the outcome of the project.

Tools for project accountability include the resource assignment matrix (RAM), which identifies each task and the level of responsibility of each party for that task. Table 8.1 provides an example of a RAM for a project task.

Table 8.1
Resource Assignment Matrix

Task 1.1	Project Manager	Senior Analyst	Human Resource Manager	Project Sponsor
1.1. Creation of recruiting materials for project team	Identify staffing requirements. Review documents prepared by HR.	Document technical skills necessary.	Create internal posting documents and advertisements.	Approve establishment of positions and grant authority to hire.

If project roles and responsibilities are not identified and documented, frustration will inevitably result. Functional managers will be distressed over the erosion of their authority and may covertly fight the project manager. Project managers will also become frustrated with the lack of clarity about their role and their inability to get things done. Senior managers must be involved enough to ensure that project managers have enough organizational power to do their job.

The Relationship between Projects and Processes

Long before the large-scale adoption of *project* management methods as a means of increasing organizational effectiveness and efficiency, mechanisms for better management of organizational *processes* were available and widely applied. Total quality management, continuous quality improvement, Kaizen, the cost of quality, re-engineering and process redesign, and most recently Six Sigma have been invested in and applied to many organizations with results that for the most part have been good.

Today's focus on projects doesn't mean that we should abandon our efforts to improve organizational processes. Indeed, an initiative to improve a process is a project that can benefit from the application of sound project management principles.

Some organizations are more repeatable-process-oriented or dominated than others. Manufacturing organizations and those organizations that process transactions are highly dependent on the efficiency of their processes. Some organizations are more project-oriented. Examples of project-oriented organizations are legal firms, consulting firms, and construction firms.

Every organization, however, has a mix of both projects and processes, though the mix is different for each. As a result, there is a close synergy between project management and process improvement. Processes can be improved with strong and effective project management, and project management can benefit from the tools applied to process improvement.

Indeed, one could argue that the application of effective project management is an attempt to apply sound and repeatable processes to the management of projects. The development of lessons learned and the application of standard project management methods and tools are to a great extent the systematization of project management. They apply documented, standardized, and continuously improved processes to the management of projects.

Table 8.2 illustrates the interfaces between project management and process improvement for a project designed to build and implement an automated information system.

Table 8.2
Interfaces between Project Management and Process Improvement
For an Automated Information System Design and Installation

Project Management Process Group	Project Management Activities	Process Improvement Activities
Initiate	Select projects. Create project charter. Identify constraints. Identify assumptions.	Identify "as is" state. Identify "to be" state. Consider alternatives. Choose solution.
Plan	Define project scope. Identify activities. Sequence activities. Develop the schedule. Identify and plan for risk. Identify quality standards. Estimate costs. Build the project plan.	Identify requirements. Document requirements.
Execute	Perform project work. Distribute information.	Design the system. Build the system.
Control	Monitor and control time. Monitor and control costs. Monitor and control risks. Monitor performance. Make changes. Verify scope acceptance.	Compare results to plans. Ensure user acceptance.
Close	Close the project.	File system documentation.

A natural tension can be expected between those who plan and manage projects and those who create, manage, and improve processes. Well-managed, that tension can provide a dynamic synergy between these two inseparable and critical organizational functions.

Functional versus Projectized Organizations

Three general types of organizational structures—functional organizations, matrix organizations, and projectized organizations—are described in the project management literature.

Functional organizations are organized around standard functional or business activities. Examples are organizations with accounting, product development, sales, information technology, and marketing functions divided into departments or business units. In a functional organization, staff report to functional managers and only participate in projects on part-time or temporary assignments. In this type of organization, the project manager has little ability to draw on the best staff for projects, has limited ability to reward or punish staff for project performance, and is handicapped by the allegiance of the project team to their "real" jobs. Most organizations are still functionally organized.

In a functional organization, project managers need to have strong skills in the following:

- Negotiations in order to negotiate with functional managers for the necessary resources
- Diplomacy in order to soothe the fears of others and get things done without having the necessary authority
- Motivating staff without having the ability to offer rewards or apply punishments

> Projectized organizations are rare. Chances are that your organization is either functional or a mix of a projectized and functional organization.

A projectized organization is almost wholly organized around the performance of projects. Examples of this type of organization are accounting firms, consulting firms, engineering firms, and law firms. In this type of organization, staff is assigned directly to project work and is rewarded for their contributions to those projects. Project managers have extensive authority and project management as a career path is highly regarded and rewarded. Projectized organizations tend to be at higher levels of project management maturity than functional organizations.

In a projectized organization, project managers need to be able to do these things:

- Manage their resources
- Motivate staff
- Delegate
- Plan the project
- Execute the plan and deliver project results

Matrix organizations provide a combination of the two. In strong matrix organization, project managers have greater authority than in weak matrix organizations.

In truth, project managers have little ability to change the structure of the organization and have to learn to cope with the form of organization that exists. In most cases they will have less authority than they might desire or think adequate. If

it were easy to manage projects and if project managers had clearly defined authority, project success rates would be high and organizations wouldn't need to invest
time and money in project management initiatives.

Project Management Offices

Some organizations seek to superimpose the application of project management methods and tools by establishing a project management office or PMO.

> Though PMOs can be very useful, there may be as many failed PMOs as
> successful ones.

PMOs can accomplish a number of useful functions such as:

- Managing critical projects or the organization's project managers.
  In this model of a PMO, project managers work for the PMO and are
  assigned to projects by the PMO manager. In some cases, only high-risk,
  high-cost projects are assigned to the PMO while simpler projects are
  allowed to be managed by the performing unit (i.e., the organization
  that will implement and use the project).

- Coordinating the projects of the organization as a portfolio of projects.
  In this model, the PMO helps assist the organization select and prioritize projects. The PMO may then perform a coordinative role between
  and among projects.

- Establishing project management standards and processes.
  In this model, the PMO is responsible for the creation and implementation of project management processes. It ensures standardization across
  the organization, sometimes fighting the development of local standards
  and practices. The PMO may also establish certification programs and
  standards for the organization.

- Providing resources to project managers.
  In this model, the PMO serves as a centralized repository of resources for
  project managers. The PMO may compile templates and best practices,
  which may be made available electronically to the other project managers.

- Providing project management mentoring services.
  In this model, the PMO provides advice and assistance to other project
  managers.

Table 8.3 describes and compares the variations among types of PMOs. The strong PMO model corresponds most directly to the projectized form of organization described above.

Table 8.3
PMO Variations

	Strong PMO Model	Mixed Model	Weak PMO Model
PMO Role	Manage key projects. Manage project portfolio. Assist in project selection.	Manage some projects. Provide resources.	Provide resources and mentoring. Develop training programs. Identify best practices.
Organizational Model	Hands-on, direct management of projects (Commander)	Combination of functions	Service provider to other project managers (Librarian)
Primary Client	Project stakeholders	Senior managers	Project managers
Personnel and Resources	Permanently assigned Significant resources	Mix of permanently and temporarily assigned staff Some resources	Few assigned resources Reliance on limited staff and volunteers
Project Management Standards	Developed and applied	Developed for others to apply	Suggested standards or best practices
Project Management Software Standards	Mandated and applied Enterprise-wide standard	Mandated enterprise or desktop standard	Suggested
Oversight of Project Managers and Teams	Complete responsibility Able to reward and sanction managers and team members Able to coordinate resources across projects	Some authority over project managers and team members Able to recommend rewards and sanctions Some ability to coordinate resources	No authority over project managers and team members No ability to sanction or reward No coordinative ability

The choice of a PMO model depends on the needs and structure of the organization. Whichever model is chosen, the role of the PMO should be made clear to those who staff it and to the remainder of the organization.

The PMO that has been established without clarity on its role and purpose can flounder and as soon as the first budget cut comes along may be abolished. Without clear definition of the role of the PMO, PMO managers are left in a vacuum without an idea of what they are supposed to do. When PMOs are established by senior-level fiat, they can be resented by the project managers they are supposed to assist.

PMOs can serve the organization well, though the project management landscape is littered with PMOs that fail to satisfy their stakeholders. To have a chance at success, they need, like the best projects, to have a clearly defined and limited scope.

Committees and Review Boards

In order to manage and govern projects, it may be useful to establish committees or review boards for a variety of purposes including:

- Evaluating potential projects and prioritizing existing projects
- Managing project changes

Unfortunately, many organizations avoid the tough task of applying selection techniques to potential projects or prioritizing projects. Having a formal selection process requires that some potential projects be rejected; disciplined project prioritization implies that some projects will be assigned a lower priority than others. It's easier, at one level, to let everyone assume that their projects are worthy of investment and that their projects are the most important to the organization. To correct these deficiencies, which will ultimately cause great harm, a project selection and prioritization committee may be established to gather stakeholder input and build consensus about potential projects.

For large projects, change requests should be documented, and once documented, need to be reviewed and either accepted or denied. Changes might include the following:

- Scope changes
- Requirement changes
- Resource changes
- Regulation or policy changes
- Schedule changes
- Cost changes

Frequently a sizable group of stakeholders needs to be involved in those decisions. In order to facilitate the necessary discussion among stakeholders, a change control board can be established. That board may include subject matter experts who can provide expert judgment on the alternatives available for meeting project needs. The board must be able to respond in a timely manner, which requires a careful balance between broad representation of stakeholders and operating efficiency.

Not all changes need to be approved by the change control board. Small changes of no consequence to the project's scope or the product of the project can be accomplished by the project team. The change management committee should create standard templates for documenting the impact of proposed changes and submitting changes to the board for consideration. To inform its decision making, the committee should ensure that they are provided the following items by the project manager:

- Project identification data, since the board may manage changes across many projects
- Date tracking, including the date submitted and the date by which is decision is required
- The reason for the proposed change, including impact on the project if the change is not made and the impact if it is
- The proposed solution

Summary and Conclusions

Without an organizational commitment to project management and an organizational structure to support it, the project management initiative is likely to grind to a halt amid frustration and dashed hopes. To make the project management initiative successful, the organization needs to create incentives for project managers, make clear to functional managers the need to cooperate with project managers, give project team members the time to participate in projects and relief from their functional duties, assign the best resources of the organization to key projects, and identify the interface among projects and processes.

A number of organizational strategies are available to encourage and support the project management initiative. First, the authority of project managers and other stakeholders needs to be made very clear. If the organization decides to employ a PMO, it must identify the role for that PMO from among the several alternatives available. In addition, the organization may identify committees that are assigned specific project management functions, like change management.

No matter which organizational form is selected, a project management initiative will impact the organization in a variety of ways, some of which will be clear and others more subtle. If the organization recognizes the changes necessary and makes those changes, the result can be both better project management and a better functioning organization.

Jump-Starting the Project Initiative
Organizational Structure

- Examine the history of project management implementation in your organization and identify lessons that can be learned from it.
- Determine the level of management and staff commitment to the project management improvement initiative. If it's low, slow down and find out why.
- Assess the extent to which functional managers are willing to allow project managers to assume project responsibility. Make sure that everyone in the organization has a common definition of project management.
- If functional managers are reluctant to share authority or have misgivings about project management, start with a pilot project and demonstrate results.
- Determine whether you have a functional or projectized organization or a mix. Match project manager training to the skills required by the type of organization (functional, matrix, projectized).
- Don't attempt to create a PMO unless you have identified its purpose and see a clear purpose for one.
- Identify your governance structure for projects and the organizational arrangements you have created for it.

CHAPTER 9

Knowledge Management and the Establishment of Project Management Communities of Practice

It's one thing to bring solid project management knowledge to an organization. It's quite another to disseminate that knowledge, put it to use, and maintain that level of competence through the twists and turns of organizational life. People come and go; the organization shifts its resources, and the knowledge necessary for effective management of the organization's projects changes.

Whether your organization is in the manufacturing or services industries, knowledge is the most important organizational resource in this information age. While competitors can duplicate all of the other assets of an organization, only the knowledge held by individuals and the organization collectively make it unique. For almost all organizations, knowledge is the key to innovation in service provision and product creation. As a result, the key to organizational survival in a complex and demanding environment is to build necessary knowledge through the process of organizational learning.

Project management knowledge as described throughout this book is a core organizational competency, and building and maintaining that knowledge is a challenge. Even if skills are presented to managers, some will fail to apply those skills, some will leave the organization and take that knowledge with them, and others will not share their new-found knowledge. Over time, that knowledge will cease to be of use. Often knowledge embedded in the heads of key managers cannot be transmitted to successive employee generations. As the baby boom generation retires, the continuity of organizational knowledge in project management will be disrupted unless there is a concerted effort to train, mentor, and coach younger workers.

Because of resource constraints, organizations need to make use of natural and simple mechanisms to leverage the competencies of key staff and build new skills sets. They need to harness the natural ability of the organization to transfer and build knowledge. If they fail, the project management initiative will not gain enough of a toe-hold in the organization to sustain the investment in project management. If they succeed in creating and managing project management knowledge, the initiative will have jump-started the development of competencies that can be sustained.

> There is no more important function of an organization than building and managing its knowledge assets.

In this chapter, we will examine the tools for ensuring that the project management knowledge gained by the organization is sustained and built upon. We'll look at the challenges of knowledge management, examine one special case of knowledge management called "continuity management," and examine the power of communities of practice, an essential factor in spreading project management through the organization and enlisting support for it.

Knowledge Management

A number of authors have recognized the key role of knowledge and continuity management in creating effective and sustainable organizations.[5] Knowledge management, which emerged in the early 1990s as a tool for organizational growth before being associated with information technology designed to increase collaboration and information sharing, is reemerging with a more human face. That reemergence has been driven by recognition that intellectual capital is hidden among the assets of an organization, that a better understanding and management of knowledge can produce dramatic bottom-line results, and that other management techniques could only go so far without careful attention to knowledge assets.

Effective learning requires both explicit and tacit mechanisms for knowledge transfer.[6] Explicit knowledge is transmittable in formal, systematic language. Tacit learning is personal, context-specific, and hard to formalize and communicate. While explicit learning can be transferred via training programs, manuals,

---

[5] Good descriptions of the importance of knowledge management and its practice can be found in Ikujuro Nonaka and Hirotaka Takeuchi, *The Knowledge Creating Company*. New York: Oxford University Press, 1995, and Thomas A. Stewart, *Intellectual Capital, the New Wealth of Organization*. New York: Currency, Doubleday, 1997.

[6] Nonaka and Takeuchi, *The Knowledge Creating Company*.

and documentation, tacit learning requires face-to-face interaction and is very much related to the context within which the knowledge will be applied.

In the project management initiative, explicit knowledge transfer can be used to make stakeholders aware of the initiative, build processes and procedures, train staff, and report on the status of the project. Explicit knowledge transfer mechanisms include newsletters, presentations, status reports, project documentation, training programs, job descriptions, manuals, and the application of standardized processes and tools. Most managers are adept at explicit knowledge transfer; it is typically one-way communication from senior levels to lower levels of the organization.

> Explicit knowledge can be transmitted through mechanisms like manuals and newsletters. Tacit knowledge requires that the knowledge be transferred person to person.

However, there are some things about project management that can't be learned from a manual; some things require direct experience, collaboration, and an evolving understanding of it. This knowledge is best acquired by exposure to working project managers.

Tacit knowledge transfer is required for that knowledge exchange, but unfortunately it is more difficult to transmit than explicit knowledge and requires a relationship of trust and a two-way dialogue. In the project management initiative, mechanisms for the tacit transfer of knowledge might include mentoring, workshops, social events, and the fostering of communities of practice, which is described in more detail later in this chapter. Tacit knowledge transfer requires informal contact and a willingness to share information and will help the organization place the project management initiative within the context of daily operations.

In order to build the intellectual capital of the organization in project management, it is necessary to create a plan that makes use of tacit and explicit mechanisms.

Continuity Management

The problems of knowledge transfer between employee generations (referred to as continuity management) are particularly difficult in an era in which turnover is rapid, and necessary skill sets are changing quickly. Today, fewer employees than before stay within the same organization for an extended period, either by their choice or their employer's. They change jobs and careers, advance to different positions that require different skills, transfer to other parts of the organization, or are down-sized, laid-off, early retired, or fired.

> Creating project management knowledge in an organization is tough; keeping it there is even tougher.

In addition, if the organization is rapidly changing, the skills necessary for success are constantly shifting. Not only are employees leaving the organization, but skill-sets have a shorter lifespan before they are eclipsed by new skill requirements.

These normal difficulties of continuity management are exacerbated today by the looming retirement of the baby boom generation. Put simply, years of experience and embedded knowledge will in a fairly short time walk out the door in disturbing numbers. In many organizations, that potential loss of knowledge represents the greatest challenge to the ability of the organization to continue to function.

In most organizations, a transfer of leadership and management responsibilities will happen whether or not those organizations or the individuals in them are prepared for it. When the most experienced project managers leave, organizations dependent on skilled project managers may find themselves being forced to rely on the project management "second team." Unfortunately, few organizations have taken the time or spent the resources necessary to build that team to a level of acceptable competence.

> Because of the increasing importance of projects in driving organizational success, it's necessary to have a strong project management "first team," "second team," and often a strong "third team."

There are a number of mechanisms that organizations can employ to offset the damage caused by the loss of key knowledge. First, they can make sure that critical knowledge is redundant. Essential knowledge should be available to the organization from more than one source. Structural capital can be stored in several systems, and information systems can be backed up. For project management knowledge, project information can be placed into a project management information system that makes it available across the organization. For human capital, the organization can cross-train its managers and work to establish deep project management expertise that can survive the departure of key managers.

Organizations can also plan for departures. An essential element of a risk management plan is the analysis of the risk that key staff persons or managers may leave. For the project management initiative, the organization should assume turnover among managers. That will require training that reaches deeper into the organization than might have been otherwise considered.

Organizations also need to develop succession planning programs that are specifically targeted toward transferring the knowledge of senior managers to younger managers. Mentoring programs, as discussed earlier in this book, can provide a mechanism for the transfer of knowledge and wisdom between employees and between employee generations. They can energize staff nearing retirement to pass on their legacy to younger managers.

For the younger managers, mentoring can provide the types of contact that can pass on tacit knowledge. If organizations begin to convert tacit knowledge to explicit knowledge, some of the knowledge contained within the heads of senior managers can be documented and converted into shareable documents like standard procedures.

Communities of Practice

In each organization, no matter what its mission or product, knowledge is disseminated by formal and informal means. We are all familiar with the formal structures of knowledge transfer like meetings, presentations, training, procedures, and mission statements.

Equally important are the informal mechanisms for information dissemination. Underneath the formal structures of the organization are informal communities that arise on their own and operate for the most part under the management radar. "Communities of practice" (abbreviated as CoP) is the term applied to those informal structures.[7]

> There are actually two organizations operating inside each organization. One is the organization that is established and managed by those at the top. The other, which may be more important, is the organization that is built by the daily practices of people throughout the organization. The two may be very different.

---

[7] The seminal work on communities of practice can be found in Etienne Wenger, *Communities of Practice: Learning, Meaning and Identity*. Cambridge, UK: Cambridge University Press, 1998.

If project management is to take root in the organization and if the organization is to create the ability to continue to grow and learn in project management, it must develop a community of adherents. Those individuals with an interest in and commitment to project management will form the basis of organizational learning. That community will extend across the organization and likely cross organizational boundaries. It may even reach outside the organization.

CoPs can also increase employee satisfaction and retention but cannot be mandated or directed. They can be fostered and energized by managers. CoPs interact around the common pursuit of problems, embody a store of knowledge, and are impeded by too much formal structure. It is easier to nurture and expand existing CoP's than to establish new ones. They require a challenge and some autonomy, which is closely aligned with the needs of knowledge workers who thrive on freedom and intellectual challenge. They hold together as long as the CoP helps them address some perceived need.

Learning is personally and organizationally transformative only if it involves membership in those informal CoPs. Rarely can an individual make substantial change in an organization by himself or herself. Nor can an individual substantially change himself or herself without the support of a community. In short, it takes a community to make change. Sometimes those communities can be formally established and operated. More often, the communities that induce organizational change and personal change are informal and emergent, that is, they emerge on their own.

In most cases, organizations overlook the usefulness of those communities. Learning communities often cross organizational boundaries. Accountants, for example, participate in CoPs that are in part formal (the AICPA) but are in large part informal (the communication between two accountants) or mixed (local associations that sponsor dinner discussions). That accounting CoP extends outside the boundaries of the organization that employs the accountant.

Managers often distrust that which they cannot control or that which they did not create. To overlook the operation of CoPs, which exist in every organization, is to miss out on their potential to create and disseminate project management knowledge and practice and to underestimate their contribution to the organization's culture.

> Though managers can inspire change, it also has to emerge from the bottom of the organization.

Looked at another way, communities of practice are clusters of professionals united by a common vision and a specific area of expertise. This is a question that helps identify CoPs: In an area I know quite a lot about, who do I talk to or ask for advice? The area might be very complex or very simple. Membership in a CoP is voluntary. Non-functional members are simply dropped. Members are free to give what they can to the community and to take from it what they need.

For an example of a CoP, think of the way that computers were introduced into the workplace. Senior managers may have made an initial investment in training and equipment, but the initiative was given energy and sustained by individuals at all levels of the organization who saw the value of computers and developed an interest in them. In almost every office or unit, there was the person who could be relied on for assistance and information. In time, those individuals found one another and an informal but self-sustaining community was formed.

Organizations and their employees can facilitate the operation of CoPs in these ways:

- Recognizing their existence and rewarding people for their participation
- Providing the members of the CoP with resources and space, either electronic or physical
- Giving them a challenge
- Understanding the unique needs of knowledge workers (challenge and intellectual stimulation)

As project management is introduced into an organization, a CoP should develop around it, and support of the CoP should be built into the scope of the project management initiative. The CoP may be started by those who first receive training in project management, or it may be started by current project managers. If successful, the CoP will serve as a resource and support network for project managers. That project management CoP can easily extend outside the organization as well if project managers participate in national and local associations. These mechanisms can help sustain the project management initiative long after the formal program has been completed.

> Managers cannot mandate participation in a community of practice, but they can provide incentives for them.

These are steps to consider for fostering and energizing a project management CoP:

- Identifying management intentions and general rules of CoP operation, including identification of potential participants
- Building rewards for CoP participation into HR processes and job descriptions if possible
- (Knowledge workers value freedom, the chance to work on exciting things, and meeting challenges.)
- Identifying existing CoPs and the potential to build on them
- (Nurturing and expanding CoPs is easier than establishing new ones.)
- Examining the role and potential for existing or new professional associations
- Holding an exploratory meeting with potential CoP leaders and members to gather input and suggestions
- Setting challenging goals for the CoP in dialogue between potential members and management

On a more practical level, managers or employees can begin to facilitate the creation of conceptual frameworks around which dialogue will occur. The dialogue will become more intense as conceptual frameworks become more clearly defined. Examples include using metaphors to help better define a certain problem or problem area, encouraging the "beginner's mind" by allowing any and all suggestions, and continuing the discussion by continuing to identify new frameworks and metaphors.

Organizations also must identify resources available to the CoP (time, space, electronic or physical resource materials, and training opportunities) and begin to involve members in wider communities of practice (e.g., area project management communities) and professional associations. Lastly, establishing evaluative criteria for the success of the CoP will help to maintain the dialogue.

> Much of the culture of the organization is embedded in informal mechanisms like CoPs.

That CoP will also go a long way towards creating a culture of project management in the organization. If the CoP is reinforced with the top-level commitment of the organization, the culture of the organization will align to the project management intentions of its leadership.

Summary and Conclusions

Knowledge management is necessary to spread the word of the project management initiative, to build support for it, and to sustain it. Formal and informal mechanisms exist for the acquiring, disseminating, storing, and managing knowledge.

Of particular concern is sustaining project management knowledge and skills from one employee generation to the next, particularly in an environment of rapid turnover and the looming retirement bubble. Without continuity management, the project management can lose steam and the results may disappear in a short time.

CoPs are a necessary but usually overlooked component of knowledge management and dissemination. To be most effective, those communities have to emerge on their own, though they can be fostered by senior managers. For some managers, CoPs are troublesome in that they cannot be managed or controlled like formal organizational structures. Given the right guidance and space, CoPs can create a self-sustaining energy that will ensure the success of project management initiatives.

Jump-Starting the Project Initiative Knowledge Management
• Identify the critical project management knowledge present in the organization.
• Ensure that knowledge transfer mechanisms address both explicit and tacit knowledge.
• Assess the risk of a "continuity" problem (e.g., number of key personnel eligible to retire).
• Build mechanisms for documenting critical knowledge and sharing it.
• Identify and examine the current communities of practice.
• Identify leaders who can serve as hubs of communities of practice.
• Set aside time and space for the development of communities of practice.

CHAPTER 10

Managing Change and Creating Long-Lasting Project Management Capability

How many times have your projects been blindsided by unforeseen change and adversity? Why is it that what looks like a great idea on paper and in the project plan is resisted by those it was intended to help?

For example, imagine a project to put a tablet PC in the hands of a social worker. With it, they can access a family's history while they work with the family. They can determine eligibility for services and register the family for services on the spot. They can access a database of resources from the family's home. They can rid themselves of that pesky paperwork that normally prevents them from spending time doing what they have been trained to do—to help those in need.

It sounds like a great idea. But imagine the reactions of those social workers to the project. They may conclude that the tablet PC is being provided to improve their efficiency and that it will be followed by an increased caseload or reduced numbers of caseworkers. They may fear that they will be unable to cope with the technology and lose their jobs; they did, after all, select a career that maximizes human contact rather than contact with technology. They may fear that the PC will cause suspicion among those they are trying to serve and diminish their ability to interact with families. Their fear and adversity, which the project manager may never have expected, may be substantial enough to cause the project to fail.

By definition, projects create change, and the initiative (i.e., project) designed to improve the project management capability of the organization is no exception. As a result, it will encounter resistance to change and all of the challenges of creating organizational change.

In addition project managers are always at the cutting edge of organizational change. They bear much of the responsibility for managing the human and process dynamics of the change created by their projects. The project manager and the person responsible for identifying and managing the project requirements (usually the project manager or a business analyst) operate at the user interface where the change will be most keenly and personally felt and most vigorously resisted.

It is never easy to create or manage change, and project managers may underestimate the resistance that their projects will create. They may presume that a good idea expressed in a clearly defined project charter will be embraced by all of the stakeholders. But if they fail to communicate effectively and constantly, if they don't address the fears and emotions of stakeholders, or if they underestimate the extent of the change they are creating and its impact on others, their projects will run into resistance and may fail to produce outcomes that satisfy users.

> Creating project plans is easy. Managing change is hard.

Failure to manage the change inherent in a project management initiative will lead to the same resistance to change as other projects. It will also cause the benefits of improved project management to be short-lived and poorly disseminated across the organization. Because of the changes in roles required by the establishment of a project management program and the threats it may imply for functional managers, change management is especially crucial to the initiative to improve project management capability.

In our earlier discussion of project communications, we discussed the fact that people affected by change react both intellectually and emotionally. In this chapter, we will examine the adversity to change that may attend a project management initiative and discuss change in a more comprehensive way. We will examine a standard change model and effective strategies for creating change, including managing grief and denial and creating new mental models. Last, we'll identify the elements of a comprehensive change management program.

Barriers to Organizational Change

We would all agree that improving the organization's capacity to manage projects is a good idea. Having laid out the potential benefits to those in the organization, it is hard to imagine that anyone could be opposed to a positive change in the way that projects are managed. Yet adversity will surely plague the attempt even though overt hostility to it may not be publicly and directly expressed.

Why? What could cause the organization or the people within it to refuse to line up and enthusiastically support the effort? What could they possibly fear?

There are always strong forces at play in every organization that impede change. Viewed positively, those forces protect the organization from unwise or destructive change. Viewed negatively, those forces prevent the organization from making the changes that will make it successful. Today, in an economic environment characterized by rapid and relentless change, the management of those forces can make the difference between successful organizations and those that lose their relevance and fail.

> Given the considerable impediments to organizational change, it's a wonder that any organizations survive.

In this section, we will detail some of the factors that might cause adversity to a project management initiative. Some of those barriers operate at the psychological level for the organization and the individual. Barriers to improving the organization's ability to manage projects include the following:

- Fear of loss of control or status
- Organizational inertia and a fixation with existing task performance
- Fear of accountability
- Experience with past, failed initiatives
- Organizational immune systems
- The expectation of failure
- Faulty mental models
- Ineffective or counter-productive reward systems

The Fear of Loss of Control or Status

One of the most effective aspects of project management is that it makes the project manager responsible for producing results. That project manager must have the ability to do things like identify resources, assign tasks, and develop project plans.

> Project management can shake the foundations of an organization. Expect some managers and staff to fear the introduction of it.

Existing functional managers may not want to give up control to project managers and may regard the project management initiative as a threat to their positions and authority. That fear may be reflected in less-than-full management cooperation with the project management initiative. Existing functional managers may become passive-aggressive, giving verbal support to efforts to improve the project management capability of the organization while attempting to frustrate it behind the scenes.

With control in an organization usually comes status. A project management program will naturally elevate the status of project managers. If status is viewed as a "zero-sum game," the status acquired by project managers will result in a perceived loss of status for functional managers.

Sometimes, the fear of loss of control will be manifested in the unwillingness of senior managers to clarify the scope of the project management initiative. Project managers may find themselves lamenting, "They claim that they want to improve project management here but they won't tell me what I'm supposed to do or tell me what authority I have." Those project managers may feel that they are being placed in a situation of trying to move projects forward but trying to guess whether senior management is committed to project management or not.

Organizational Inertia and Fixation with Existing Task Performance

Changing an organization is much like turning a very large ship while it is underway. It takes time and only happens gradually.

A project management initiative requires fundamental change in the way an organization operates. Not only will the formal structures like processes, structures, and skills need to change, but the organizational culture will need to be changed as well. That culture will need to shift in these ways:

- From hierarchical structures to project structures
- From diffuse accountability to clear accountability
- From traditional indications of status (e.g. office size and permanent resources) to outcome-based status
- From activity-based performance assessment to assessment based on project outcomes
- From stability to constant change

Organizational inertia will slow any organizational change initiative. People are comfortable with existing routines, have learned them over time and have been successful, to some extent at least, by applying the old models. Often for no better reason than "we've always done it that way," people will resist change.

> Inertia can be good for an organization because it can prevent bad ideas from disrupting operations. But it can also impede necessary change.

Change also requires that the resources of the organization be realigned. In the minds of managers, project-driven reallocation of money and staff will likely imply winners and losers, at least until the benefits of better project management begin to be realized and it becomes clear that more resources will be made available throughout the organization. Being a loser of resources reduces power, flexibility, and the ability to accomplish goals. It is no wonder that any initiative that promises long-term results but costs money in the short run is vigorously challenged.

Sometimes, people can get so immersed in the details of their work that they can't see the need to break that task cycle to make improvements. A good metaphor for this type of behavior is the lumberjack who can't take a break from chopping to sharpen his axe even though doing so would help him to cut down more trees.

People find comfort in repetitive action and stability. Stakeholders who, though they might support the project, fail to find the time to dedicate to the project or free up resources from other, daily tasks, may be exhibiting the comfortable anesthesia of repetitive task performance.

Fear of Accountability

Good project management clearly identifies the responsibilities of the manager, team members, and stakeholders. In addition, a good project management methodology identifies metrics for the measurement of project success. In most circumstances that might be regarded as positive.

However, organizations and individuals may see project management as a tool that could expose their failures. For example, many organizations don't track project costs. A project management initiative that begins to identify costs and measure project progress against the budget can identify failures on the part of project managers just as easily as success. If managers not are confident in their ability to accomplish results, it is less threatening to them to operate in an environment that doesn't hold people accountable. Accountability can be a fearsome thing.

Any initiative that establishes new metrics requires fundamental changes in the behavior of those in the organization. An organization that has existed without metrics has effectively measured the ability on the part of managers to create the impression (rather than the reality) of performance. If a project management initiative includes, as it should, metrics for measuring the success and failure of projects, it will experience resistance.

Experience with Past, Failed Initiatives

The project management initiative is probably not the first time that the organization has tried to improve its effectiveness. A cynical person might regard it as the "management tool d' jour." It may be following initiatives like total quality management, re-engineering, and management by objectives, which, though they may have been successful, have come and gone. Those initiatives may not have fully accomplished their advertised potential.

> Some people in the organization may try to wait out the project management initiative in the belief that things will eventually get back to normal.

It is natural that people in most organizations are skeptical of improvement initiatives. Their past experiences may also be coupled with distrust of management in general. Often people assume that their managers have hidden agendas—agendas that will ultimately benefit the managers but not themselves. That may especially be the case if managers are employing project management in order to better utilize resources.

Organizational Immune Systems

Human beings are not comfortable with change. As a result, they have the ability to construct "immune systems" that allow them to deny the fact that change is coming. The "boiled frog" syndrome is a common metaphor for this type of human reaction. In that often-cited but, one would hope, poorly researched case, a frog in a pan of water will not notice the gradual increase in the temperature of the water until it is too late.

Denial is the chief manifestation of immune systems. Rationalization is its principal tool.

Some argue that people have such well-developed denial systems that they can only be induced to change by the realization that they have no choice but to change and that grievous harm will befall them if they don't change.

The Expectation of Failure

Sometimes people adopt a belief system that convinces them that any organizational change will have bad results for them. That belief system is built on past experiences and a cycle of slow recovery from adversity. Breaking that cycle requires the development of strategies to establish rapid, positive movement that displaces negative expectations with positive experiences.

> It's hard to change people's minds when they are convinced, beyond logic, that project management won't work or that it will work to their disadvantage.

The project manager will see the expectation of failure in action in those persons who are certain, despite any evidence to the contrary, that the project is certain to affect them negatively. No matter how may positive messages about the project are delivered, those who have learned to be victims will assume the worst and sometimes poison those around them with their negative interpretations.

Faulty Mental Models

Human beings also cloud their vision by viewing the future through the lens of experiences of the past. Human beings are also "order seeking," in that they attempt to find models that simplify the complexity of their lives. Having found a model that they are comfortable with, they look for evidence, even when that evidence may be lacking, to confirm their model and prove its correctness. Making effective change requires breaking the patterns of those embedded models and replacing them with models that work better in the current circumstances.

Project managers encounter flawed mental models in the argument that "the way we've done it in the past is the best." Sometimes, the project team can exhibit poor mental models when they become wedded to a particular technology or solution. As a result, change is difficult because we try to apply the same tools to analyze and solve every problem—tools which bias us toward only limited behavior patterns and processes.

> There is an adage that when the only tool you have is a hammer, every problem looks like a nail. That's true of project management and the management methods it will supplant.

Changing mental models is tough. People usually don't willingly give up the mental models that have, so they think, served them well in the past. It is like convincing the scientists of the pre-Columbus world that the world is not flat. People in the organization have made an investment in the system that is being replaced by learning it and improving it over time. It will be hard for them to give up on something that they feel ownership in.

Ineffective or Counter-Productive Reward Systems

Most organizations don't reward people for taking chances and often provide rewards for those who avoid risk and operate within standard and traditional patterns. Often penalties are levied on those who take chances and make mistakes.

The reward systems of the organization are often beyond the reach of project managers, particularly in functional organizations. Often they have to do the best they can with the modest rewards at their disposal. Without the ability to reward good project behavior or punish those who fail to deliver, project managers operate with one hand tied behind their backs.

The lack of good reward systems is complicated by organizational structures that encourage siloing of units and functions. Without strong incentives to share resources and participate in organization-wide initiatives, unit managers may simply opt out of participation in projects. Their adversity may not be overt but may be manifest in their inability to find the resources to devote to project assignments. Too frequently, an initiative to increase the project management capacity of an organization founders because subordinate units simply refuse to play along.

The Standard Change Model

The standard model employed by most managers for attempting to create change in organizations has not been very effective. Typically, they identify the need for change through some sort of analysis, devise a solution, and attempt to convince stakeholders of the need for the adoption of the solution through an appeal to their intelligence. (Even worse, sometimes managers find a tool that they like and look for a problem to apply it to.) Sometimes they are successful, but often they are not. The reality of the workplace is that emotion as well as intellect determines the reactions of the organization and stakeholders to the change. Those emotional reactions can cause potent adversity.

Faced with failure and having not achieved buy-in from the stakeholders, the change agent attempts to marshal the force to compel the change. Unable to convince stakeholders to buy in, the change agent will resort to force, mandates from more senior managers, and office politics. Unfortunately, the common reaction to an attempt to force change is even more resistance and more failure. Ultimately, failure becomes clear and the focus shifts to finding someone to blame. Figure 10.1 illustrates the standard, ineffective model managers usually apply to create change.

Figure 10.1
The Standard Change Model

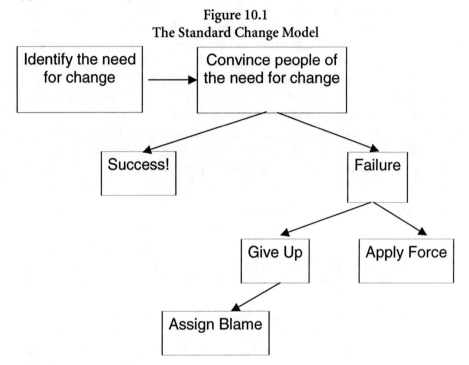

Effective Change Management Tools

Effective change requires a combination of strategies that addresses the emotional impact of change and replaces old behavior patterns with more effective mental models. In this section, we will consider the management of emotional reactions to change and building new mental models.

Coping with Grief and Denial

Though we usually associate grief only with death, grief is an unavoidable reaction to any uncontrollable change. Grief in the workplace may be the result of a change in a process, a change in a pattern of communications, resource reductions, turnover, or new job duties, all of which all will be present in a project improvement initiative. Grief allows people to buy the time necessary to adjust to the change and cycles through a known pattern of emotions, from denial to ultimate acceptance. We can't prevent grief from occurring, but we can recognize its impacts and manage those impacts embedded in the grief cycle.[8]

If managing the reactions of stakeholders as they work through the grief cycle were not tough enough, different people will move through the cycle at different speeds. When that occurs, conflict will result. Those who have moved to anger will have little tolerance for those who are still in denial. Those who have completed the cycle and have accepted the change will be unable to understand those who are left behind. In creating organizational change, the most difficult stage to address in the cycle is denial.

> The first and most difficult step in creating change is convincing people that change needs to occur and getting past their denial.

Fortunately, there are strategies for combating the natural denial that will result from an attempt to create change. First, the need for the change must be demonstrated clearly. The need can't be based on opinions and presumptions but on clear analysis and evidence. In the presentation of the need for change, the project manager may need to rely on the trust that he or she has built up in the organization.

However, intellectual arguments and logic, no matter how carefully presented, can go only so far. The natural and predictable emotional reactions of stakeholders to change must also be addressed. Identifying the likely fears and threats to stakeholder interests is required. Change can also be facilitated by identifying those in the organization who are looked to as leaders as well as those who are most likely to adopt the change. Last, the project manager has to create a clear path toward the change and build excitement among participants.

Ultimately, the challenge of the project manager is to replace the negativity and fear of change with a compelling vision of a new, better future.

---

[8] The most highly regarded work on the grief process is Elisabeth Kubler-Ross, *On Death and Dying.* New York: Touchstone, 1969.

Building New Mental Models and Systems Thinking

As noted earlier, a major factor in our inability to recognize the need for change is our propensity to view the future through the lens of the past. It is very hard to see new patterns and new models because we have been preconditioned by our history and our experiences. In order to create change, we need to get at the root causes of our problems. Addressing those root causes will have a far more favorable impact on the problem than simply addressing symptoms.

The goal of looking at problems with "new eyes" is to replace old mental models, which may no longer fit the environment, with new models that do. That may require that we look for the lack of fit between models and reality and that we examine conflict for indication of the lack of fit.

"Systems thinking" is a technique that attempts to describe the dynamic relationships that influence complex systems. The goal is to identify the relationships within the system and the root causes of problems. With those in mind, solutions can be designed that address real problems rather than symptoms.

Changing mental models is tough on even the smallest issues. We have to be persistent in our attempt to encourage change, identify those who can help us lead change, provide solid evidence of the need for change, and realize that change may not come as fast as we expect.

Creating a Comprehensive Change Strategy

As indicated earlier and throughout this chapter, the creation of an effective change strategy requires a balance of intellectual arguments and rational design with an understanding of the emotional needs of our stakeholders. It requires that we not engage in wishful thinking that the people we are dealing with had different emotions and different tolerances for change. We have to create change where we are with the people we have.

> Designing an effective change strategy requires that we take a long, hard and honest look at the organization and at ourselves.

Effective change strategies require that we build big changes on little successes. There is no greater change imperative than to build trust among those affected by the change, and there is no better way to build trust than to demonstrate success.

It also requires that we involve people in the changes that will affect them. Recall that we described grief as a reaction to *uncontrollable* change. Giving people the ability to control some of the change they will face is an effective change strategy that also combats the natural human fear of the unknown.

In the face of change, we need to communicate often and in varied ways. Some people gather enough information from written explanations of the change, some prefer meetings, and some require face-to-face communication. Our natural propensity is to communicate with stakeholders less when change occurs and when risk goes up. In truth, we need to communicate more.

Creating a comprehensive change strategy is the most effective way to manage change and overcome the resistance to the project management improvement initiative. The following table (Table 10.1) provides an illustrative set of strategies. The plan for each organization, of course, must be crafted based on its unique circumstances.

Table 10.1

Strategies for Overcoming Barriers to Change

Barrier to Change	Symptoms	Strategies
Lack of understanding of the value of project management	Skepticism about the initiative Lack of support Lack of willingness to consider the program	Create a clear business case in terms managers use. Present research on the value of project management.
Denial of the need for the initiative	Senior management cynicism Reluctance to invest in the initiative Reliance on "the way we always do things" Skepticism with "just another management fad"	Identify change leaders and early adopters. Address solutions to real organizational "pain points." Tailor messages to respond to fear factors. Communicate in multiple ways using multiple media.
Overt opposition to the initiative	Clear opposition Conflict	Identify a champion for the initiative. Tailor messages to respond to fear factors. Engage in constructive conflict management that recognizes that all views are legitimate to those who hold them.

Barrier to Change	Symptoms	Strategies
Covert opposition to the initiative	Lack of progress coupled with a lack of conflict	Meet with those you suspect of covert opposition to identify their pains and objections. Develop solutions that address their needs.
Lack of senior-level support	Inability to get other managers to participate or share resources	Present research on the value of project management. Identify a champion.
Unclear objectives and inability to clarify them with senior managers	Poor communications with senior managers "Second guessing" project implementation	Develop a project charter and distribute it to senior managers. Identify risk factors and issues and present them to senior managers. Clarify assumptions in writing.
Limited authority or ability to affect the organization due to semi-autonomous units	Refusal or unwillingness of units to participate Inability to schedule training or orientations	Employ pilot programs. Market the benefits of project management to autonomous units. Provide an array of options that can be applied by autonomous units, rather than attempt to create a single, uniform solution. Create incentives for adoption.

Summary and Conclusions

Managing change is one of the least attended to elements of effective project management. That is unfortunate since projects create change and project managers must manage that change if their projects are to be fully successful.

Impediments to effective change abound. Projects create fear and require that people move outside their comfort zones. Their adversity to the change may be overt but also may be covert and hard to identify.

A variety of strategies exist for helping people and organizations cope with change. Application of those strategies requires good communications skills, a comprehensive approach to managing change, ability to understand the fears and needs of stakeholders, and an understanding of the natural psychological processes that create adversity to change. The very best project managers plan their projects and include plans for managing the organizational changes their

projects create. The initiative to improve an organization's project management capability is no exception.

Jump-Starting the Project Initiative Managing Change
<ul><li>Expect stakeholders to fear the project management initiative.</li><li>Build extra communications into the project plan and get creative about communicating with stakeholders.</li><li>While you're trying to change things, the organization will attempt to do things the way it always has. Give people a compelling reason to change the status quo.</li><li>Build incentives for making better use of project management.</li><li>Model the changes you expect the organization to make with your own behavior.</li><li>Be honest about the level of change that you can create.</li><li>Be patient; the change will not occur overnight.</li></ul>

Case Study: Services Firm
Improving Project Management Capabilities

A national provider of business services saw the need to improve its performance on client engagements and internal projects. Its principal goals were to create a repeatable process for managing client engagements, capture lessons learned and improve its learning processes, better identify project risks, ensure that critical project issues, like client billing, were attended to, reduce the resources dedicated to internal projects, and speed up internal projects.

After providing encouragement to several project managers to acquire their PMP® certification, most company employees were provided between four and six hours of project management orientation. Project management methods were applied to several internal projects.

The company also designated a PMP as project coordinator. The project coordinator attempted to create a project monitoring tool for identifying project status.

Despite the efforts of the coordinator, the company struggled to embrace effective project management. There was no clear definition of the duties of a project manager, and project managers dueled with functional managers. The project monitoring tool was used sporadically, and no consistency in project management was developed.

Ultimately, the role of the project coordinator was eliminated. Senior managers restarted the initiative to improve the project management capacity of the organization by encouraging still more managers to acquire their PMP certification. In addition, the role of the project manager was clarified somewhat by drawing a distinction between that role on projects and other project roles. Project managers were designated for key internal and external projects, and junior project managers were mentored by more senior managers.

Though the initiative to improve project management capabilities is ongoing, it is beginning to produce results. Most importantly, there is a growing interest in project management in the company among managers at all levels and an appreciation at senior levels of the importance and role of effective project management.

APPENDIX 1

Assessing the Organization's Project Management Maturity

Prior to embarking on the capacity development project, it would be useful to determine the current capacity of the organization to apply good project management. That assessment is often conducted using a project management maturity model.

There are a variety of maturity models available. In this appendix, we present a short-form assessment tool that can give the organization a quick idea of its maturity. This short model can be combined with individual skill assessments to provide more detail on the training needs of individual managers and can be used to pinpoint the areas most in need of improvement.

Do not lose heart when you take the assessment! Most organizations are at fairly low levels of most maturity models. Project management initiatives as described in this book can increase the level of maturity, and the fact that you are reading this book and thinking about or applying an initiative to improve your project management capacity puts you ahead of many other organizations.

Each organization must make the decision as to which level it aspires toward. In some cases, reaching the top levels of a maturity model may not make economic sense for the organization. Without question, the cost of moving to high levels is not trivial. It is clear, however, that most, if not all, organizations can improve the way they manage projects with a comprehensive approach.

Short-Form Project Management Capacity Assessment Tool

Choose the Statement that Most Closely Describes Your Organization:

I. **Project Management Expertise:**

- There is no formal project management training. Project managers are self-trained. (1 point)
- Project managers have or receive some training in project management. (2 points)
- Project managers receive extensive, formal training in PM, and PM certification or degree achievement is encouraged. (3 points)
- PM is a recognized and valued expertise. Most project managers are certified or degreed in PM. PM expertise is available to assist troubled projects, and some informal PM mentoring takes place. (4 points)
- Internal project managers are certified or degreed and actively involved in the education and training of others inside and outside the organization. Certification or advanced training in project management is required. (5 points)

II. **Project Management Methodology:**

- There are no organization-wide PM methods, tools, or procedures. Each project is managed independently without shared or common methods. PM tools are independently selected and applied by individual managers. (1 point)
- A PM methodology and tool have been selected. (2 points)
- PM tools and methods are standardized within units but may vary across the organization. (3 points)
- PM methods and tools are standardized across the organization. (4 points)
- PM methods and tools are standardized and shared across the organization, and PM templates and tools are customized to meet the needs of the organization. The organization has developed its own PM methodology based on its needs. (5 points)

III.**Assessment of Project Performance:**

- The performance of projects is not assessed. Data on project costs and schedules are not collected or analyzed. (1 point)

- Project performance is assessed informally. Some data is available. Quality criteria (i.e., how will we know if this project is successful) for each project are only informally developed. (2 points)
- Data on project performance is collected and built into project plans. Project quality criteria are identified and clearly stated in project plans. (3 points)
- Data on project performance is collected and compared across the organization. Criteria for project success are clearly communicated. (4 points)
- Managers are held accountable for project success based on measurable and clearly known criteria. Projects are managed on a portfolio basis. (5 points)

IV. Sharing Project Management Lessons and Expertise:

- No lessons learned are collected and shared. No programs for knowledge sharing have been established. Little informal sharing of lessons learned takes place. (1 point)
- Project managers informally share information and knowledge. Personal repositories of lessons learned exist. (2 points)
- Some lessons learned are retrievable with regard to past projects. (3 points)
- Sharing of PM knowledge and lessons learned is encouraged, and automated tools enhance sharing. (4 points)
- PM communities of practice exist and are encouraged. Formal systems exist for retrieval and sharing of PM knowledge from inside and outside the organization. (5 points)

V. Project Portfolio Management and Strategic Value of Project Management:

- Each project is managed as a stand-alone initiative. (1 point)
- There is some, but little, coordination among projects. PM is not integrated with organizational goals. (2 points)
- Coordination across projects exists, and PM is integrated into organizational goals. (3 points)
- A PMO or similar organization has been formed for coordination of project across the enterprise. The concept of a strategic project portfolio guides management thinking. (4 points)

- An effective PMO has been created and is in operation. The strategic direction of the organization is centered around the portfolio of projects. (5 points)

VI. **Project Scope Definition and Requirements Definition**

- Project scope is poorly defined and little scope documentation exists. There is no process for defining, building, and maintaining consensus on project scope. Project changes are not integrated into scope documentation. (1 point)

- Some effort is expended on scope definition and requirements gathering. Project charters, scope statements, and WBS are commonly used tools. A scope management process is informal but in place. (2 points)

- A formal process has been defined for gathering and documenting project requirements. The scope management process is formal and employed to make and track changes. Project changes are integrated into project scope documentation. (3 points)

- The organization employs business analysts (explicitly or functionally) to identify project scope and requirements. The organization employs methods for ensuring that requirements are clearly and accurately defined and may use a recognized process, such as rapid application development or agile methodologies, for ensuring that systems meet user requirements. (4 points)

- The organization explicitly employs business and systems analysts. Scope definition and requirements definition methods are employed consistently across the organization. (5 points)

Scoring:

Add up the total for the descriptive statements you have selected. If your score is:

      6 through 9:

Your organization is not making use of the power of professional project management and analysis. Expect most of your projects to be over budget, late, and delivered with less than fully expected functionality. Most organizations score in this range.

      10 through 15:

Your organization is making some use of project management and analysis tools. Some improvement has already likely to have been made in project performance, though project performance is likely to be mixed (some successes and some failures). With continued development, the organization can achieve even better results.

16 through 21:

Your organization has made a commitment to realizing the benefits of project management. Most projects are likely to be successful, and the organization is able to learn from project successes and the occasional failure. Improvement is still possible with continued development.

22 through 27:

Your organization has reached an advanced stage of project management maturity. You are likely realizing success on most projects and are able to strategically move the organization through the use of successful projects.

28 and Higher:

Your organization operates among a very few organizations that is project-based and committed to very high levels of project success.

APPENDIX 2

Tools for Project Selection and Prioritization

This appendix explores mathematical methods for choosing and prioritizing projects. In the world of business, a financial return on the investment in projects is required since financial success is the ultimate requirement for corporate survival. Even in the public sector, effective stewardship of public funds is required, though it is more difficult to measure the costs and benefits of public projects than it is for private sector projects.

Financial tools can be applied to the analysis of projects, much in the same way they can be used to evaluate make-versus-buy decisions or the analysis of investments. To justify the investment in a project or to rank projects, a return on the funds invested in the project can be calculated. Demonstrating that return is beset with all the challenges that attend to the cost-benefit analysis of any strategic investment, including the challenges of estimating costs and, harder still, estimating benefits.

We will consider four tools for analyzing the financial impact of projects:

- Benefit/cost ratios
- Payback
- Net present value
- Internal rate of return

Return on investment (ROI) is a generic term describing various methods for assessing the ability of the project or other investment to recoup its costs or generate a return. It is axiomatic that the benefits of a project should exceed it costs. Complications of calculating an ROI include cost and benefit estimation, calculating the impact of uncertainty, taking into account the time-value of money, and identifying risk preferences of the organization.

These tools can be applied to individual projects and to the decision to invest in a project management initiative. That initiative is a project as well.

Benefit/Cost Ratios

A benefit/cost ratio (BCR) is expressed in ratio format, as in a BCR of 3:1, which states that the benefits of the project are three times the costs. Unless benefits and costs are discounted for the time value of money (described below), BCRs can be misleading.

Payback

Payback analysis simply identifies the number of time periods required to recoup the investment in the project or asset. Payback is expressed in time periods (e.g., payback in six months or payback in three years). Payback, though simple, usually suffers from its failure to adjust flows of costs and benefits for the time value of money. In some cases an organization may set a threshold level for payback, thereby taking on projects whose payback is within acceptable limits (e.g., the organization may take on only those projects with a three-year payback or less).

For projects that recoup their investment within a very short time period, payback may be an appropriate tool for investment. Once benefits or costs are spread across several future periods, however, payback begins to exhibit perverse results. Take, for example, the following two projects.

Project	Upfront Cost	Year 1 Benefit	Year 2 Benefit	Year 3 Benefit
A	$40,000	$10,000	$10,000	$20,000
B	$40,000	$30,000	$5000	$5000

Both projects have a payback period of three years and appear, on that basis, to be equal. However, Project B is superior in that the benefits are received earlier than in Project A. To evaluate these types of cost and benefit flows, we need more sophisticated tools.

Net Present Value

Net present value (NPV) improves upon the payback method by taking into account the concept of the time value of money. That concept simply states that a dollar received at some point in the future is of less value than a dollar spent or received today. This is due to a variety of factors including inflation, uncertainty, and the cost to the organization to raise the funds necessary to fund the project (e.g., the cost of borrowing or the cost of issuing new stock). In an NPV calculation, the present value of the cash outflows related to the project (costs) is subtracted from the present value of the cash inflows (benefits). If the result is a positive number, the project is deemed to have a positive NPV and therefore to be financially advantageous.

Cash flows are discounted to their present value by application of the formula:
$PV = FV/(1+r)^n$

Where:

PV = the present value of the funds

FV = the future value of the funds

r = the interest or discount rate

n = the number of periods into the future that the flow will be achieved

For example, if the upfront project cost is $75,000 and the benefit to be gained is $100,000 to be realized two years from now, and the appropriate discount rate is eight percent, the PV of the benefits ($100,000 to be received or realized two years into the future) is $85,734, calculated as follows:

$PV = 100,000/(1 + .08)^2 = \$85,734$

In the example above, NPV would be calculated by subtracting the cost of the project ($75,000, in our example) from the discounted future benefit ($85,734). The result is positive ($10,734), and, as a result, this project could be deemed to be financially rewarding.

It is likely that benefits will be realized over several periods, and in complex projects costs may also be spread over several periods. The benefits realized in each future period and costs incurred in future periods will need to be discounted to their present value. There are techniques for computing the present value of streams of costs or benefits (for example, if the project results in annual savings to the organization of $10,000 per year for ten successive years).

In the calculation of NPV, the choice of a discount rate (r) is key. The discount rate may include an estimate of future rates of inflation as well as a factor for estimated project risk. The higher the discount rate, the greater is the difference between future value and present value. That is, if a high discount rate is applied, the present value of future flows will be lower than the present value of a similar amount at a lower discount rate.

Except under rare circumstances (expected deflation), the present value of an amount to be received or spent in the future will be lower than its future value (i.e., in our first example, the PV of $100,000 to be received in two years is only $85,734). NPV can be used to evaluate any stream of costs and benefits, such as those related to projects or those related to the purchase of assets.

Internal Rate of Return

Internal rate of return (IRR) operates on the same principles as NPV. It differs only in that it calculates the discount rate (r) at which inflows and outflows are equal. Put another way, the IRR is the discount rate at which the NPV of the project is zero (neither positive nor negative). It is expressed in percentage terms (e.g., an IRR of fifteen percent). Calculation of the IRR is more complicated than the calculation of the NPV and won't be illustrated here. Most financial calculators have the capability to calculate an IRR.

For the IRR to be useful, it has to be compared to a "threshold rate" or "hurdle rate" established by the organization. For example, an organization might set a rule that it will not undertake projects with an IRR that is less than twenty percent. A project with an IRR of fifteen percent would not be undertaken. A variety of factors is involved in the establishment of the organization's hurdle rate.

NPV and IRR are closely related. A project with an IRR less than the threshold rate will also exhibit an NPV that is negative. A project with an IRR greater than the threshold rate will exhibit a positive NPV.

978-0-595-37226-3
0-595-37226-0

Printed in the United States
100025LV00004B/394/A